MY ANCESTORS WERE FREEMEN OF THE CITY OF LON

Vivienne E Aldous

1999

Published by

Society of Genealogists
14 Charterhouse Buildings
Goswell Road
London EC1M 7BA

Registered Charity No. 233701

ISBN 1 85951 400 6

British Library Cataloguing in Publication Data

A CIP Catalogue record for this book is available from the British Library

Vivienne Aldous has worked as a professional archivist at the Corporation of London Records Office (CLRO) since 1984, the same year the city freedom admission archives were first deposited there. Before qualifying as an archivist, she worked as a volunteer at several archive repositories including the Yorkshire Archaeological Society in Leeds and Leicester Record Office. She is also an amateur genealogist and a keen gardener.

ACKNOWLEDGEMENTS

I gratefully acknowledge the help of my colleagues, past and present, at the Corporation of London Records Office, Guildhall Library and the Chamberlain's Court. Without them, this book could never have been written. I am indebted to Betty Masters and the late JFV Woodman for their various works of research, both published and unpublished, which have been such useful reference tools. Particular thanks are due to Jim Sewell, Elizabeth Scudder, Stephen Freeth, Richard Harvey and Caroline Arnold, who kindly read and commented on the draft text. Any errors or omissions which remain are purely my own. I would also like to thank Else Churchill of the Society of Genealogists' Library for her help, and John Titford for his expert assistance, especially with the bibliography. Last but definitely not least, thanks are also due to my husband Paul, for being so actively supportive and encouraging me during the compilation of this book.

All illustrations in this book are reproduced by the kind permission of the Corporation of London Records Office, except for plate X, which appears by kind permission of the Society of Genealogists.

Vivienne E Aldous
August 1998

CONTENTS

ILLUSTRATIONS

All illustrations in this book are of documents held by the Corporation of London Records Office (CLRO), and are reproduced with permission.

1
INTRODUCTION

What is the freedom of the City of London

Many people, if asked 'Was your ancestor a freeman of the city of London?' might well reply, 'Oh no, he was only an *ordinary* person. He couldn't possibly have done anything to deserve being made a freeman'. This reaction illustrates two common misconceptions about the freedom of the city of London. Firstly, it supposes that freemen of the city of London were not 'ordinary' people. Secondly, it assumes that the city freedom has to be earned by some brave or otherwise extraordinary act. Neither of these assumptions is necessarily correct. In fact, in the past 300 years, about 300,000 people, most of them ordinary working people, have become freemen of the city of London. Only a very few of them obtained the city freedom as an honour, in recognition of a deed or a career of great merit.

Other people know full well that their ancestor was indeed a freeman of the city of London. Perhaps there is a well-known family story, or a continuing tradition of members of the family becoming city freemen to this day.

Yet other people might have an ancestor's city freedom certificate: a distinctive long, thin strip of parchment, written in Latin before 1733, bearing the seal of the chamber of London, and often folded inside a small rectangular red, blue or black wallet or rolled within a cylindrical wooden box, sometimes marked 'copy of freedom' (see Plates I and II for illustrations, translation and transcripts of the wording of such certificates). They may well not know anything more than this, however, and questions may still remain as to why and how a particular ancestor became a city freeman, and what it meant at the time.

The records of freemen of the city of London, which survive in the Corporation of London Records Office (CLRO) in a more or less continuous sequence 1681-1940, can be valuable to the genealogist seeking ancestors in the 'square mile' of the city of London. From the middle ages, towns and cities strove to be self-governing and to give their citizens, or freemen, trading advantages over strangers from outside their communities. In London, which has been for so many centuries (as it still is) the largest and most important city in the kingdom, the concept of such a community developed early, and acquiring the freedom of the city of London became a necessity for those who wished to make a living within it. Immigrants

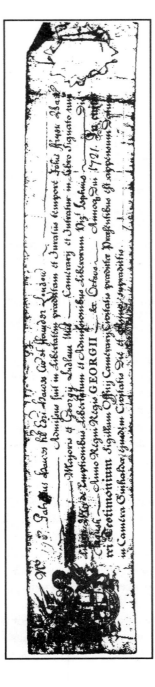

Plate I: A typical city of London freedom certificate from before 1733

Transcript

No. [1961 *Patricius Hawes fil' Edri' Hawes Civ et ffounder London*] *Admissus fuit in Libertatem predictam[or praedictam] et Juratus tempore [Johannis ffryer Bart] Majoris et [Georgii Ludlam Mil'] Camerarij et Intratur in Libro Signato cum Litera [M] de Emptionibus Libertatum et Admissionibus Liberorum Viz. [septimo] die [Augusti] Anno Regni Regis [or Reginae if a queen] George II etc. [octavo] [Annoque Domini [1721] later added] In cujus Rei Testimonium Sigillum Officij Camerarij Civitatis predicte [or praedicte] Presentibus est appensum Datum in Camera Guihaldae ejusdem Civitatis die et anno supradictis.*

Translation

No. [1961 Patrick Hawes, son of Edward Hawes Citizen and Founder of London] was admitted into the Freedom aforesaid and made the Declaration required by Law in the Mayoralty of [John Fryer, baronet] Mayor and [George Ludlam, knight] Chamberlain and is entered in the book signed with the Letter [M] relating to the Purchasing of Freedoms and the Admissions of Freemen that is to say the [7th] day of [August] in the [8th] Year of the reign of King George II and in the Year of our Lord [1721] In Witness whereof the Seal of the Office of Chamberlain of the said City is hereunto affixed Dated in the Chamber of the Guildhall of the same City the day and Year abovesaid.

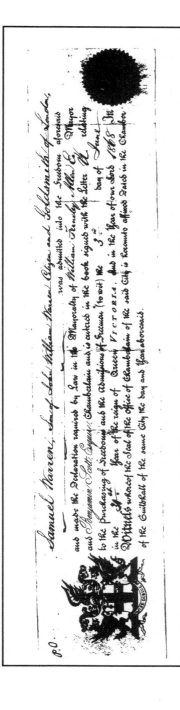

Plate II: A typical city of London freedom certificate from after 1733

Transcript

[Samuel Warren, son of John William Warren., Citizen and Goldsmith of London] was admitted into the Freedom aforesaid and made the Declaration required by Law in the Mayoralty of [William Ferneley Allen Esq] Mayor and [Benjamin Scott Esquire] Chamberlain and is entered in the book signed with the Letter [U] relating to the Purchasing of Freedoms and the Admissions of Freemen (to wit) the [3rd] day of [June] in the [31st] Year of the reign of Queen Victoria and in the Year of our Lord [1868] In Witness whereof the Seal of the Office of Chamberlain of the said City is hereunto affixed Dated in the Chamber of the Guildhall of the same City the day and Year abovesaid.

from all over the British Isles moved to London to better themselves, and the city freedom records show the enormous diversity of such people and their places of origin. By the early 19th century, this requirement to be a city freeman was being seen by some as out-of-date and burdensome, but many people trading in the city could still be prosecuted for not being a freeman until the 1850s, and so the city freedom records cover a fair cross-section of people living and working in the 'square mile' until then. Even after it ceased to be a necessary prerequisite for most people, the city freedom continued to attract (and still does attract) people who wished to be associated with the city of London in a unique way.

To put it very simply, if your ancestor worked or lived within the 'square mile' of the city of London, or had links with it, especially before the 1850s, there is a strong probability that he (or less frequently she) might have been a freeman of the city of London. In addition, before 1835, he or she would first have to have been a freeman (i.e. member) of a city livery company (as the successors to the medieval trade and craft guilds in London are known), in order to become a freeman of the city of London.

This book intends to be a practical guide, for genealogists and other users, to the records relating to freemen of the city of London and to give some of the background to the city freedom. It will describe the kind of people who had to become city freemen, the means by which they did so, the records which survive, and what information they yield about individual freemen. Wherever relevant, it will also identify other record sources associated with the freedom of the city of London. It does not attempt to cover the records of freemen of other towns and cities, which often had different rules governing admission to their particular freedom.

Before describing the freedom of the city of London and its records in more detail, it is worth looking at the context in which it flourished, and the background to the city and the people who became city freemen.

What was (and what was not) the city of London?

It is probably worth defining, to begin with, the physical boundaries of the city of London, popularly known as the 'square mile', right at the heart of metropolitan London.

On a modern map, the city of London can be seen stretching from Fleet Street and Holborn in the west to Aldgate (not including the Tower of London) in the east, and from the Thames in the south to the Barbican and Liverpool Street Station in the north. The boundaries have altered only slightly over the centuries: a substantial alteration of some of the city's external boundaries occurred in 1994, but overall the city's boundaries, and those of its parishes and wards, have not changed much from those of the 16th century.

There are a number of published facsimiles of historical maps of the city of London and its boundaries, some of which also include the later suburbs around the city, and the city of Westminster. Such facsimiles usually include street indexes. These are listed amongst the publications in appendix 1.

Much of the city of London still lies within the original Roman city walls, some of which can still be seen along the street called London Wall, for example. The medieval city of London kept more or less within the boundaries of the old Roman walls, although it did spread out a little beyond them, particularly to the north and west, giving rise to those parishes and wards which even today bear the epithet 'without' [i.e. outside the walls]. Beyond these fairly early overspill areas outside the walls, the suburbs began to grow from about the 16th century.

The borough of Southwark, just at the southern end of London Bridge, was always an important adjunct to the city, and jurisdiction over it was claimed, exercised and squabbled over for centuries. Despite the appointment of a city alderman for the ward of Bridge Without (i.e. Southwark) from 1550, however, it was never truly included within the city of London, and remained a suburb. The best book about the history and development of Southwark, with particular emphasis on its relationship with the city of London, is probably David J Johnson, *Southwark and the city* (Oxford University Press for the Corporation of London, 1969).

The Corporation of London, the local government body for the city of London, never laid serious claim to the wider suburbs, or to the city of Westminster, and so those areas were never added to the ancient city of London for administrative purposes. They remained in their ancient counties (Middlesex and Essex north of the Thames; Kent and Surrey south of it) until the establishment of the London County Council in 1889, when many of them formally became part of what we know today as metropolitan or Greater London.

Most city freemen, whilst they might have originated outside the city itself, usually lived or worked principally within it. Many did have trading and family links outside the city as well, but their chief base was the city, at least before the 1850s. People outside the city of London could and did become freemen of the city of London, especially after the 1850s, but usually only if they had personal reasons for doing so.

In the days when the freedom was a necessity, many people chose to live in the suburbs in order to avoid the trouble and expense of having to become city freemen. On the whole, it is unlikely that an 18th or early 19th century ancestor living and working in Islington, Marylebone or Bermondsey, for example, would have bothered to have been a city freeman, especially if he or she were only a small trader. However, those located in those parts of St Giles Cripplegate within the city, or in Aldgate, or Newgate Street, for example, would probably have been free.

Careful checking of known addresses of ancestors in London, and a comparison of them against a map of the city boundaries should show whether it is likely that an ancestor was a city freeman. If all the addresses skirt the outside of the city, the answer is probably no: if they form a mixture, or are mainly within the city, the answer could be yes, your ancestors might have been freemen of the city of London.

How was the city of London governed?

This might seem rather a dry, academic subject, but the government of the city was so closely bound up with the city freedom that some idea of how it worked is useful for an understanding of the city freedom. However, this section is intended to give only an outline of city government, and not a detailed picture. For further reading on this subject, see the list of publications in appendix 1.

Even after the development of the suburbs into what is now metropolitan London, the city of London remained a separate jurisdiction, maintaining administrative control over the ancient 'square mile' of the city of London, and jealously defending its ancient customs and privileges, including the city freedom.

The voters in each of the city's 26 wards (reduced to 25 in 1978, with the joining together of the wards of Bridge and Bridge Without) had to be liverymen (not just city freemen) in order to vote in Parliamentary elections 1725-1832, and freemen retained the vote in civic elections until 1867. To represent each ward, they elected one alderman and several common councilmen (i.e. councillors), the number of common councilmen varying according to the ward and the date. In 1824, for example the ward of Lime Street had 4 common councilmen, whilst Tower ward (next to, but not including the Tower of London) had 12 and Farringdon Within had 17. The total number of common councilmen for the city as a whole varied according to date, from 187 in 1549 to 234 by 1666, and 240 (its highest total) in 1826, dropping to 206 by 1840. One of the common councilmen in each ward was appointed 'deputy to the alderman' by the alderman of the ward. He was, in effect, the senior common councilman in that ward, and known as 'Mr Deputy [Smith, or

Jones or whatever]'. Every intending common councilman and alderman had to be a city freeman before he could stand for election.

Before about the late 17th century, the aldermen used to deal with the majority of day-to-day civic business, sitting as a body called the court of aldermen, presided over by the lord mayor, and which also included the recorder of London (a judge). However, during the 18th and 19th centuries particularly, the court of common council, made up of all the common councilmen and aldermen sitting together, also presided over by the lord mayor, increasingly took on most civic government, and today it undertakes all those matters which would be dealt with by any local authority anywhere in the country. Most people today think of a court as a court of law, and it is true that the court of aldermen did have a judicial role which developed into the mayor's court, but in general terms the court of aldermen and the court of common council were, and still are, administrative courts, or councils. The term is used in the same way by the city livery companies, each of which has a governing body called the court of assistants, made up of the senior members of the company.

In the context of the city freedom, it is useful to note that the court of aldermen dealt with matters appertaining to city livery companies, and city freedom admissions through them, whilst the court of common council had jurisdiction over all matters to do with the custom of London, and in particular dealt in detail with admissions to the city freedom which did not come through the city livery companies (a practice made possible only after 1835).

The other major body which used to have a much greater role in the government of the city of London than it does today is common hall. Common hall still meets each year at or close to midsummer (24 June) and Michaelmas (29 September) to elect the city of London's two sheriffs and the lord mayor respectively. It also used to elect other senior officers of the corporation, such as the chamberlain (the city's treasurer), the town clerk, the city's MPs and other municipal officers. Membership of common hall is made up of the liverymen (i.e. senior members) of the city livery companies, who consequently used to have a very large say in city affairs, and who were, especially in the 18th century, very political and vociferous.

CLRO has all surviving records of the courts of aldermen and common council, and of common hall. Fair copies of the proceedings of the courts of aldermen and common council 1275-1689 are to be found in the series of letter books, of which letter books A-L have been edited and published by RR Sharpe (see appendix 1 for details). However, the letter books were really superseded after 1416. From 1416 to date, CLRO holds the series of journals (i.e. proceedings) of the court of common council, although court of aldermen business is also recorded in the journals until 1495, when another separate series of proceedings (known as the repertories) of the court of aldermen commenced, and is still also continuing to date. All three series, the letter books, journals and repertories, have manuscript subject (but not name) indexes in CLRO, and they record the proceedings of the courts of common council and aldermen in full. Printed minutes, which are less full, exist for the court of common council from 1811 to date, and for the court of aldermen from 1853 to date, each indexed annually. The difference between journals/repertories and minutes is one of detail: for example, a letter to the relevant court will be copied out in full in the repertory or journal, but only a brief note of its receipt subject matter will normally appear in the minutes. The original letter, or other such document, put before the particular court should itself be preserved amongst the relevant minute papers (arranged by date of meeting) of common council (1643 to date, with gaps, especially earlier in the series) or of aldermen (1663 to date, with gaps, especially earlier in the series). Common hall minutes exist in CLRO 1642-1660, 1718 to date, with minute papers from 1641 to date.

What were the city livery companies?

At this point it is probably worth explaining what the city livery companies were, as they too interlink almost inextricably with the city freedom. Before 1835, every person applying to become free of the city first had to be a freeman (i.e. a member) of one of the city livery companies. This company freedom was separate from the freedom of the city.

The city livery companies had their origin in the medieval trade and craft guilds of the city. Guilds existed in most medieval cities and boroughs, although only the city of London still has so many active livery companies, there being 100 companies at present (1998), some of them very recently established. Guilds and companies outside London are listed, with brief historical and other details, in RF Lane's *The outwith London guilds of Great Britain* (see appendix 1 for details). The medieval guilds existed essentially to protect their members' interests, and could be powerful lobbying groups for their craft or trade. In theory, they also set standards of workmanship, and inspected the work being turned out in their craft to ensure proper quality control. They often had a religious role before the reformation of the 16th century, and even after that, they effectively acted as friendly societies, taking care of elderly or infirm members and their orphans, and looking after members who had fallen on hard times. Many city of London livery companies set up almshouses and schools which still exist, such as the Haberdashers' Aske's School, Hertfordshire. The livery companies were not medieval trade unions, nor does modern trade unionism have any direct links with the livery companies or guilds, except that both types of organisation have a welfare role akin to the friendly societies.

To a large extent, the city of London livery companies' day-to-day control of their trades broke down during and after the 16th century, although most retained their welfare and charitable roles. Increasingly after this time, the livery companies' membership ceased to be made up purely of people following the companies' original trades. In some ways, this was an obvious development of having a system which included admission to the freedom by patrimony: for example, a man's son might have a right to join his father's livery company by patrimony, even though he did not follow the same working trade as his father. By the early 19th century, few companies had a strong trade or occupational link. This can mislead or puzzle the researcher who is not used to the written conventions. A typical example is that of Paul Storr, the famous 18th century silversmith, who was a freeman of the Vintners' Company, as well as of the city of London, and was therefore a 'Citizen and Vintner of London'. This stock phrase, 'Citizen and [something] of London' announces to the researcher a person's freedom of the city of London and of one of its livery companies, but not necessarily his or her actual occupation. Paul Storr was never a working vintner and, for some reason, did not become a freeman of the most obvious livery company for his occupation, which was the Goldsmiths' Company. This situation is very common, and having an ancestor described as a 'Citizen and Wheelwright of London' does not necessarily mean that he or she made wheels for a living. Some livery companies, such as the Wheelwrights' and the Spectaclemakers' Companies in the early 19th century, seem to have attracted large numbers of members from every kind of occupation, perhaps because they were cheaper and easier to join than many of the others.

From the 1870s, particularly following the report of the royal commission on livery companies in 1884, the city livery companies experienced an upsurge in membership, and many of them rediscovered or re-emphasised their trade and craft roots, and are today active in promoting them.

Generally speaking, there are two levels of membership of most city livery companies: the company freedom and the livery. Ordinary members are known as freemen of the company, and this is a completely separate freedom to the freedom of the city. Senior livery company members are known as liverymen, and are entitled to wear the livery, or distinctive robes, of their company. Each company's master (or prime warden, as he is known in some companies) and wardens are elected annually from the company's court of assistants, the members of which are liverymen and form the governing body of the company. In order to become a liveryman of a company, a person must first be a freeman both of the company and of the city of London. Before 1835, anyone wishing to become a city freeman first had to become a freeman of one of the livery companies, and is therefore said to have been admitted to the city freedom through, or in, that particular company. After 1835, it became possible to be admitted to the city freedom without first being a company freeman, although many people continued to be admitted through a company. A person who had become a city freeman after 1835, not through a livery company, could subsequently join a livery company and have their company freedom recorded in the chamberlain's court at Guildhall. Such recordings are usually annotated in the alphabets (i.e. indexes) of city freedom admissions in CLRO.

The court of aldermen is responsible for regulating the city livery companies, and also for recognising new ones, which it still does from time to time, the newest being the Information Technologists' Company, the one hundredth city livery company, which received its grant of livery in 1992. Before receiving letters patent under the mayoralty seal allowing it to become a full livery company, an aspiring company has to spend several years as a company without livery. There are still two 'ancient' companies which have never been granted a livery, and therefore have no liverymen. These are the Parish Clerks' Company and the Watermen and Lightermen's Company. A person could not become a freeman of the city through one of these companies. For further details about working watermen and lightermen, see the section on them in chapter 2. The 'ancient' companies are those founded before the 20th century, the youngest of them being the Fanmakers' Company, created in 1709.

There is an order of precedence of the city livery companies, and the most senior ones form a group known as the 'great twelve'. A complete alphabetical list of all the companies, including the number of each in the order of precedence, and the whereabouts of their records, appears at appendix 2. Before 1742, the lord mayor always had to be, by tradition, a member of one of the 'great twelve' livery companies. If he was not, he had to transfer his membership, or 'translate', from his minor livery company to one of the great twelve. Translation from one livery company to another was (and is) also possible for people who wished simply to switch membership, although both livery companies involved had to agree to the translation, and it had to be sanctioned by the court of aldermen. Translations were not common, however, and decreased from the late 18th century, when people began to be members of more than one livery company. By the late 19th century, some individuals belonged to half a dozen or more livery companies, one of which (usually the first one joined) was known as the 'mother company'. One can still only belong to *one* of the 'great twelve' companies, however, even if one belongs to several of the minor companies.

Most of the city livery companies have deposited their archives in the Manuscripts Section of Guildhall Library (see appendix 2 for a list of these, together with the whereabouts of those records not in Guildhall Library). In some cases, the information to be found in the livery company archives will not add much to what is in the city freedom archives, although sometimes they will include actual occupations, addresses or other information lacking in the city freedom admission papers. In cases where a person was not free of the city through a livery company (only possible after 1835), they will not help at all, of course. However, anyone becoming free of the company or city by apprenticeship (known as 'servitude' in the city) would also have had their apprenticeship binding recorded by their company at its outset. Not all apprentices necessarily completed their terms of apprenticeship, and whilst some might have become freemen of their company, they might not have gone on to become freemen of the city as well. In addition, there are some gaps in the city freedom records, particularly for the late 17th and late 18th centuries. The livery company archives, therefore, can be a useful adjunct to the city freedom records.

A number of livery companies' apprentice bindings have been extracted from the companies' records by Cliff Webb and published by the Society of Genealogists (SoG). Most livery companies have printed histories, many of which include lists of masters, wardens and clerks, and some of which include lists of apprentices and freemen. SA Raymond's book, *Londoners' occupations*, lists many of these books, and gives details of other useful bibliographies. There are also various published lists of company apprentices and freemen for some of the city livery companies (see appendix 1). The Society of Genealogists also has various unpublished manuscript and typescript lists and indexes of company apprentices, freemen, liverymen, masters, clerks and the like, a select number of which appear in appendix 1.

A list of the liverymen and freemen of some of the city livery companies who signed the association oath rolls pledging allegiance to King William III in 1696 was prepared for publication in about the early 1920s, probably by Wallace Gandy and JH Bloom. It included the names of the wardens, assistants, liverymen and freemen of companies beginning with the letters A-F (Apothecaries- Fruiterers) (see appendix 1 for details). Although the book was never finally published, the proofs, with manuscript annotations and a more modern typescript index, are held by the Society of Genealogists' library, and copies are held at Guildhall Library and CLRO. The original association oath rolls 1695-96, including rolls for London other than the ones signed by members of the livery companies mentioned above, are held in the Public Record Office (class C 213). They are described in 'The association oath rolls of 1695' by Cliff Webb in the *Genealogists' Magazine*, Vol. 21, no. 4 (December 1983). Some local association oath rolls have been edited and published, and details of these, plus the whereabouts of locally held rolls, are detailed in Jeremy Gibson's *The hearth tax and other later Stuart tax lists and the association oath rolls* (see appendix 1 for details).

Freemen of the city and of livery companies might also be included in Boyd's *Inhabitants of London* (formerly also known as Boyd's *London Citizens*) which is held by the SoG (see appendix 5 for details).

City companies should always have held their meetings, including those at which apprentices were bound, in the city of London. However, the Framework Knitters' Company appears to have held court meetings in Nottingham in 1727, while the company's register of freedom admissions 1713-24 in Guildhall Library Manuscripts Section covers some freedom admissions made in Nottingham, Leicester (rather fewer) and Hinckley, Leicestershire (fewer still). Under one of the Hinckley entries is a note:

'Memorandum. There has been noe Acco[un]t of any admittances from Leicester or Hinckley to London but these four entered here, viz. [names follow] (being now sent up by the Deputies [to] Mr ffoster, Cl[erk] in their last half yeares Acco[un]t to Xmas 1720) since ye sixth of May 1718, page 116'.[1]

The Company was obviously, therefore, admitting some freemen locally in the Midlands, and then forwarding details to the clerk in London, although this must have been rare amongst the companies, and was probably not very common even within the Framework Knitters' Company. It is probably explained by the fact that historically (and to this day), the main areas of framework knitting, and hosiery production in particular, outside London have always been Nottinghamshire and Leicestershire, with centres at Nottingham, Leicester and Hinckley.

2
WHO HAD TO BE A CITY FREEMAN AND WHY?

For anyone making a living within the city of London, the city freedom was an important requirement. From the middle ages, the city corporation issued orders that only city freemen were allowed to operate within the city as retail traders, brokers, and licensed victuallers, for example, and there were strict prohibitions against masters employing non-free journeymen without licence from the corporation. A city tradesman who was not a city freeman could find himself presented by his neighbours at the local wardmote (a meeting of inhabitants of a city ward) for not being free, and if he did not take up the city freedom promptly, the Corporation of London could (and often did) prosecute him. Likewise, liverymen of the city livery companies had to be free both of their company and of the city of London.

Rights and privileges

Before the Reform Act of 1832, only freemen of the city of London were allowed to vote in municipal elections in the city, and only liverymen could vote in parliamentary elections. After 1832, inhabitant householders and occupiers of the annual value of £10 who were not necessarily freemen could also vote, although city freemen retained the right to vote in municipal elections purely because they were freemen until 1867, when the right was finally abolished. Liverymen of city companies, however, were allowed to vote until 1918 and could still do so until 1948 if they also possessed a business qualification to vote, and they appear separately listed in the registers of electors. CLRO has city of London parliamentary registers 1840, 1872 to date (with gaps), whilst Guildhall Library has them covering 1832 to date (with fewer gaps). Both CLRO and Guildhall Library also have copies of ward registers (listing those entitled to vote in municipal elections in the city) 1950 to date, whilst in addition CLRO has registers for a few wards 1946/47-48/49. The common hall registers list those liverymen entitled to vote at common hall for the lord mayor, sheriffs, and, historically, other officers too. Again, both CLRO and Guildhall Library have copies of Common Hall Registers 1887/88 to date (1940-41 missing).

Before secret ballots became the usual form of voting, electors' votes were recorded in poll books. CLRO also holds some poll books and scrutiny books for particular elections in the city of London 1712-1823 (with gaps). These are listed in more detail in appendix 3. The whereabouts of poll books for the city of London held at

CLRO and elsewhere are listed in *Poll books c1696-1872: a directory to holdings in Great Britain*, edited by Jeremy Gibson and Colin Rogers (see appendix 1 for details). London voters polled in the general election of 1713 have been published by the London Record Society in London pollbooks, 1713, edited by WA Speck and WA Gray (see appendix 1 for details).

Another important privilege held by city freemen from the middle ages until the 19th century was their exemption from having to pay market tolls anywhere in the country, or tolls on animals coming into the city's markets to be sold. This latter exemption, on animals driven into the city for sale at market, has led to the famous city myth of freemen having the right to drive sheep (or cattle, or other animals, depending on the version of the myth) over London Bridge. No doubt anyone trying this today would find themselves swiftly falling foul of modern-day traffic laws. However, it shows how urban myths can sometimes be founded on a kernel of truth.

The Corporation of London was very assiduous in defending the rights of city freemen to be exempt from tolls and dues elsewhere in the country, and there are references in the journals (i.e. proceedings) of the court of common council in CLRO to the corporation defending or supporting court actions on behalf of citizens of London. The journals are subject indexed (not name indexed) and it is possible to check through the subject indexes under the heading of 'tolls' and discover the names of the persons involved in such cases. The year 1801, for example, saw the end of a ten-year-long case against the Corporation of Liverpool over port dues charged on 'Messrs Freeland, Ryan and others', freemen of London, but resident in Liverpool, and a summary report on the case was reported to common council.[2] Such summary reports, and references to progress of such cases, are certainly easier to find, and to understand, than any records of legal proceedings themselves might be.

City freemen were also technically exempt from naval impressment, which must have been very valuable in the days of the Napoleonic wars, when the naval press gangs were abducting hundreds of men a year to serve as sailors.

Another legal privilege which city freemen held was the right to be tried in the city's own courts of law. This was a valuable right to merchants, who often traded within the jurisdiction of many courts outside the city. There were technical aspects of business law, in particular, in former times which made cases heard in the mayor's court of the city of London useful to the London businessman.

Under the custom of London, a city freeman's personal property at death was divided into thirds. One third went to the widow, another third was equally divided between the children, whilst the final third could be disposed of in the freeman's will. The court of orphans, presided over by the common serjeant, had custody of any under-age orphans of freemen and supervised the administration of the personal (but not real) estate of the late freeman. As a result, an inventory was made of all the personal property of deceased freemen who left children who were minors. Land, being real rather than personal property, is not included in the inventories, but they usually include a detailed description of the contents of the freeman's house, room by room, together with any stock in trade, debts owing to and by the freeman, and the like. CLRO has over 2,000 such orphans' inventories dating about 1662-1742, 1764-73, with indexes.

From medieval times, city freemen also had the right to hunt in Middlesex, although again, this right has been defunct for a very long time.

Besides the sheep over London Bridge, there are a number of other civic myths (all of them quite false) which claim to be legal privileges of city freemen. These range from the privilege of being executed with a silken rope, or beheaded with a sword rather than an axe, to the 'right' of urinating against cart-wheels with impunity. The first two are clearly irrelevant today, whilst indulgence in the last would, like the herding of sheep over London Bridge, no doubt bring the swift attention of the police.

Elderly city freemen and their wives, widows or daughters, were also eligible for admission into the City of London Freemen's Almshouses (formerly the Reform and then the London Almshouses) at Ferndale Road, Brixton, which the corporation acquired in 1848, although candidates for admission did not have to be city freemen by the 20th century.

The orphans of city freemen were eligible for admission as foundation scholars to the City of London Freemen's School, which was opened as the city of London Freemen's Orphan School in 1854, although a few children were admitted at the very end of 1853. From 1924, the orphans of female freemen had the same right of admission. A maximum of two orphans of any freeman's family could be admitted, although occasionally, in particular cases, an extra child might be admitted. The school was co-educational from the beginning, and fee-paying boy pupils (not necessarily the orphans, or even children of city freemen) were admitted from 1926, when the school changed its name to the City of London Freemen's School and moved from its original site in Brixton to its present one at Ashtead, Surrey. Paying girl pupils were admitted from 1933. CLRO has pupil records of the Freemen's School 1853-1955 (75 year closure period), as well as an excellent set of detailed application forms for both boys and girls 1853-1943 (75 year closure period). The application forms name the child and the mother or guardian who is petitioning for admission. They also give the name of the free parent (usually the father), and their freedom admission date, date of death, and former occupation. The number and ages of other children in the family are also routinely given, and it is noted whether any other children within the family are already at the school, or whether any of them are already working. Details of the mother's employment and income are also noted.

Poor widows of freemen were also entitled to apply for 'widows' tickets', a certain number of which were allocated for distribution by aldermen and common councilmen. The widows presented their tickets at the chamberlain's office in Guildhall, and obtained a small allowance.

City of London sworn brokers

City of London sworn, or licensed, brokers had to be freemen of the city from the middle ages until 1856, and even after that date, some brokers continued to become freemen. The corporation had been given a royal charter in 1285 permitting them to license all brokers, defined historically as any middle man or agent in any trade, operating in the city. In theory, this included brokers on the Stock Exchange, but from the late 18th century it became common for brokers actively to avoid being sworn, on principle, and to challenge the corporation's right to license them. From 1697, the corporation administered the licensed brokers under various Acts of Parliament, the numbers of Jewish and alien (non-British) brokers being limited in number to twelve each, with a further twelve allowed from the refugee Protestant Dutch and French churches. CLRO has fairly full records of sworn brokers from 1697 until the corporation lost the right to license them in 1886. These records include bonds of licensed brokers and their sureties for good behaviour 1697-1870 (indexed), and registers of brokers admitted 1708-1869, and admitted, discharged and died 1772-1886. CLRO publishes a free leaflet giving more details about the city sworn brokers, which can be supplied by post on receipt of an A5 stamped, self-addressed envelope.

City licensed victuallers (publicans)

Licensed victuallers, including those running public houses, in the city of London also had to be city freemen before they could hold a licence until 1856. However, relatively few records survive of them as such beyond the city freedom admission papers. CLRO has victuallers' licences, arranged by wards 1683/4-mid 18th century (with a very few up to 1857) but then no records of licences at all until a new series of comprehensive licensing registers commences in 1873. None is name indexed. The earlier victuallers' licences tend to give only the ward, the date of the licence (they were usually renewed annually in March) and the licensee's name. The pub name is virtually never given before 1873, nor is any personal information about the licensee, which is why it is so useful that they had to be city freemen before 1856. The licensing registers after 1873 give more information, including the licensee's and owner's names, dates of holding the licence, and the name and address of the licensed premises, but by then licensees did not need to be city freemen, and often were not.

To cover the earlier period, and the effective gap in records at CLRO between the mid 18th century and 1873, perhaps the best source is the city trade and post office directories, a good set of which is held by Guildhall Library.

Licensed non-freemen working as journeymen in the city

On a practical basis, only allowing city freemen to work in the city had its drawbacks. It meant that, in order to work in the city, ordinary people had to spend a comparatively large sum of money to join a livery company and pay the city freedom admission fees. Many people chose to live outside the city rather than do this. This lack of skilled labour was also problematic for businesses in the city, so the corporation allowed a certain number of non-free journeymen (people who had served an apprenticeship, but who worked for a wage for someone else, rather than had their own business and apprentices), provided that they were licensed by the corporation.

CLRO has licence books (10 volumes) for these non-free journeymen 1750-1845, indexed for both masters and journeymen 1750-61 and for masters only 1761-1810.

The lord mayor, aldermen, sheriffs and common councilmen

As mentioned in chapter 1, anyone wishing to stand for election as a common councilman, alderman (including the lord mayor) or sheriff of the city of London first had to be a city freeman, and this is still true today. The corporation was usually strict in ensuring this. Odd examples of this rule being broken do turn up from time to time, and one appears below, in the section on oddities in chapter 7.

Aldermen from the earliest times up to 1913 are all listed and indexed, with some biographical information, in AB Beaven, *The aldermen of the city of London* (London, 2 volumes, 1908, 1913). CLRO has full indexes up to the present day to all aldermen since Beaven's book, as well as to all city lord mayors and sheriffs. CLRO also has indexes to common councilmen up to the present day, although for common councilmen of the 18th century and earlier there might be some errors and omissions in the index. In addition, CLRO holds copies of the corporation pocket books from 1788 to date (with gaps, especially in the earlier period), which were published annually and which list the names, addresses, wards and committee service of each common councilman and alderman for each year. Biographical details of aldermen and common councilmen are published in JR Woodhead, *The rulers of London 1660-1689* (London and Middlesex Archaeological Society, 1965).

Some of the better-known lord mayors, sheriffs, aldermen and common councilmen are the subject of biographical entries in the *Dictionary of national biography* (*DNB*), a new edition of which is currently in preparation. Some are also included in F Boase, *Modern English biography* (1892-1921, reprinted 1965) or *Who was who 1897-1980* (7 volumes, published by A and C Black, London, 1929-1982, with a *Cumulative index ... 1897-1980*, (1991)). The *DNB* and *Who was who* are also available on CD ROM. Many (but by no means all) are the subjects of biographical notes, compiled by archivists in CLRO on a fairly *ad hoc* basis over the past thirty years or so. These vary in content and length from very full to very sketchy (dates of office, perhaps a parent's name, an address, etc.). If you have an ancestor who fits into this category, especially if he were well known either in city or national circles, it is always worth checking with CLRO, to see if there are existing biographical notes.

Another useful source is Guildhall Library's Noble Collection, a set of very variable notes on many city figures, some including detailed genealogical notes, others containing a bare précis of a person's career. There is sometimes an overlap between Guildhall Library's Noble Collection and CLRO's biographical notes.

Guildhall Library also has microfilms of the city's local newspaper, the *City Press* (later the *City Recorder*) from 1857, and *The Times* [1785 to date], as well as some other London newspapers. These often cover elections and admissions of sheriffs and lord mayors and major civic events involving them, such as royal entertainments. The more famous characters will also have obituaries in *The Times*, which has published quarterly indexes, as well as a cumulative index to 1920 on CD ROM, also held by Guildhall Library. The less famous characters usually have an obituary in the *City Press*, which is not indexed, so a date of death needs to be known before a sensible search can be made. Many more newspapers are held by the British Library Newspaper Library.

Corporation employees

People who worked for the corporation as employees theoretically had to be city freemen until 1987 if they earned above particular salary grades, the level of which varied from time to time. However, it had been impossible, both legally and in practice, to insist upon this for some time before its formal abolition, as admission to the freedom required the payment of a fee. Nevertheless, many staff members above the lowest grades did become city freemen and many continue to do so. Corporation employees worked at a variety of different locations in various departments, not just at Guildhall itself, the corporation's headquarters in the city of London. Not everyone is aware that these other departments (listed below) were or still are run by the Corporation of London:

Some Corporation of London departments at locations outside Guildhall

Corporation of London schools:

City of London School (established 1834);
City of London Freemen's School (established as the City of London Freemen's Orphan School in 1854, name changed in 1926);
City of London School for Girls (opened 1894);
Guildhall School of Music and Drama (established as the Guildhall School of Music, 1880).

Corporation of London open spaces outside the city:

Epping Forest (acquired by the corporation in 1878);
Burnham Beeches (acquired by the corporation in 1880);
Coulsdon Commons, Surrey (acquired by the corporation in 1883 and added to since: includes Coulsdon Common, Riddlesdown, Kenley Common and Farthingdown);

West Wickham Common, Kent (acquired by the corporation in 1892, and added to since);
Highgate Wood and Queen's Park, Kilburn (acquired by the corporation in 1886);
West Ham Park (acquired by the corporation in 1874).

Corporation markets:

Billingsgate Market (probably in existence since the 10th century);
Leadenhall Market (probably in existence since the 14th century, acquired by the corporation in the 15th century);
Smithfield Market (now officially the London Central Markets, probably in existence since the 12th century);
Metropolitan Cattle Market (removed from Smithfield to Islington in 1855, closed 1939);
Foreign Cattle Market, Deptford (1872-1914);
Spitalfields Market (acquired by the corporation 1901 (freehold) and 1920 (leasehold)).

Other corporation establishments:

City of London Mental Hospital (established as the City of London Lunatic Asylum in 1866, passed to the National Health Service in 1948), Dartford, Kent;
Tower Bridge (opened 1894).

CLRO holds the surviving staff records of these departments, although these records exist mainly from the late 18th, 19th and 20th centuries only, and may be patchy. Any surviving records of market tenants and porters at the various markets, mainly for the 19th century, and City of London Mental Hospital patients 1866-1948 are also in CLRO, although the latter are closed by law for 100 years. Such records are listed in appendix 3. CLRO does not have any records of individuals who worked on the construction of Tower Bridge, as the construction work was undertaken by a number of contractors. Surviving records of corporation staff who were employed on Tower Bridge after it was opened can be found in CLRO, but this can involve lengthy research through committee minutes, and it helps if the dates of employment are known.

CLRO has lists and details of corporation officers, the easiest to consult being the printed returns of 1879, 1886 and 1908, which list, but do not index, officers department by department, and give details of the duties, salary, and length of service of each officer named. There are also other returns of officers, mainly for the late 18th-20th centuries, in CLRO. There is also a fairly detailed list of corporation offices (not including the names of office-holders, however), with job descriptions, in the *Second report of the royal commission into municipal corporations in England and Wales: London and Southwark, 1837.*

Porters

Porters in the city of London should also have been city freemen, particularly if they belonged to one of the organisations which regulated porters of various kinds in the city under the general administration of the Corporation of London. Each type of porter had particular duties and privileges and demarcation disputes between the different kinds of porters were not uncommon. The best book about London porters and their various organisations is Walter M Stern's *The porters of London* (listed in appendix 1).

The Billingsgate Porters, also known as the Fellowship Porters or the Coal, Corn and Salt Porters, had a monopoly in the porterage of measurable goods (including coal, corn, salt, and fruit). These measurable goods were defined by a royal charter to the Corporation of London in 1605, although the corporation's right of metage (the right to levy dues on measurable goods entering the city) was far older than that. The corporation appointed officers called meters to collect the necessary duty payable on certain of these measurable commodities, most notably coal, corn and fruit, which were loaded and unloaded by the Fellowship Porters. The governor of the fellowship was always the alderman for the ward of Billingsgate, although he tended to leave the administration of the organisation to the deputy governor, who was always the deputy of the ward of Billingsgate, together with the fellowship's ruling body. The Fellowship Porters were wound up as an organisation in 1894, and their surviving archives (including membership lists between about 1845 and 1891) are held by the Manuscripts Section of Guildhall Library.

The Tacklehouse and Ticket (formerly street) Porters were established as a united society by the corporation in 1609. Tacklehouse porters, usually twelve in number, operated from the great twelve livery companies' waterside tacklehouses, and were high-status porterage contractors, employing ticket porters to work for them. Their enforced amalgamation with the ticket (or street) porters in the early 17th century created a rather incongruous body, but it lasted until about the 1870s, when it finally petered out. Again, the organisation's archives are held by the Manuscripts Section of Guildhall Library, and include membership lists 1604, 1673-1869.

Porters of aliens' goods, or alien porters, were employed by the city's packer and porter of aliens' goods (also known as the city packer), who leased that office from the Corporation of London. He was responsible for the collection of the duties of package, scavage, balliage and porterage for the corporation and administered the licensing of the porters he employed, who should have been city freemen. Records of porters employed would have been kept by individual city packers, and do not survive at CLRO, although the records of the court of aldermen include details of the leasing of the office of city packer. The government purchased the Corporation of London's rights to the package, scavage, balliage and porterage duties by an act of parliament of 1833 (3 & 4 Wm. IV, cap. 66), after which the corporation lost its administration of alien porters.

Watermen and lightermen

Working watermen and lightermen (carrying passengers and cargo respectively) on the Thames were, in theory, obliged to be city freemen in order to work, as well as to be members of the Watermen and Lightermen's Company. In order to become a freeman of the city before 1835, a person had first to be a freeman of a city livery company. However, because the Watermen and Lightermen's company was not a full livery company, not having received a formal grant of livery, people had to become fee of the city through another company, and so they appear in the alphabets of city freedom admissions as being admitted through a company other than the Watermen and Lightermen.

People who did not need to be free: king's freemen

Soldiers and sailors who had served in HM Forces, and their families, were permitted to exercise trades on their discharge, 'notwithstanding local bylaws' which otherwise banned them from doing so. There were three acts of parliament under which this was allowed: 24 Geo III, Sess. 2, cap. 6 (1784, repealed 1871), 42 Geo III, cap. 69 (1801/2, repealed 1872) and 56 Geo III, cap 77 (1816, repealed 1873). Deserters were not included in the acts. In the city of London, the particular 'local bylaw' which was circumvented by the acts was the requirement that only city freemen could trade within the city, and so the discharged servicemen who took advantage of them were rather misleadingly known as 'king's freemen', although they were not actually freemen of any description. In order to trade within the city of London without being a freeman, the discharged serviceman or his family had to obtain a certificate of entitlement from the chamberlain, which prevented the city's officers from harassing the holder of the certificate, who was otherwise liable to be prosecuted for being a non-free trader. In order to obtain the certificate of entitlement, the ex-serviceman's discharge certificate, and sometimes other documents, had to be produced to the chamberlain. About 4,000 sets of 'king's freemen's' discharge papers survive for the late 18th to early 19th centuries in CLRO, with an index. The discharge certificates give details of the relevant military or naval service, and there is sometimes a physical description of the serviceman, and the name of the hospital, if the ex-serviceman were a pensioner. If the person applying for the certificate of entitlement was a member of the ex-serviceman's family, then the papers sometimes include certificates of marriage or baptism. The main snag about these papers is that they are in very poor physical condition. However, the slip index in CLRO extracts most of the information contained in the papers themselves.

3
HOW PEOPLE BECAME FREE

Age

All freemen have to be 21 years of age or above, even today. A city bye-law of 27 September 1556 ordered that no-one was to be admitted to the city freedom before the age of 24, but this requirement did not last, or was probably not observed. Certainly by the late 17th century, from when records of freedom admissions survive in quantity, the minimum age of admission was 21, and a large proportion of freemen were admitted at that age, although some were much older.

In the fourteen years during which the present author has had experience of the city freedom admission papers, only one person has come to light who is known to have become a city freeman under the age of 21. He was Germaine Lavie, born on 30 March 1730/31 in Lagor, France, and naturalised in 1749, who became a city freeman in January 1749/50 at the age of 19, probably due to his wealthy and influential city connections.[3]

On the whole, searches for city freemen whose date of admission is unknown should usually start at the date of their supposed 21st birthday, although it is sometimes worth searching from a few years before this date, especially if the only evidence of the person's age is a date of baptism.

Sex

The city freedom has always been open to women as well as men, although not always on the same basis, and historically there were far fewer female than male freemen. Women who were free of the city used to be known as 'free sisters', a term now only maintained by some of the city livery companies for their own female freemen. Up until 1923, the only women who could become free of the city were spinsters and widows: married women could not do so. If a spinster or widow who had become a city freeman subsequently married, then her city freedom went into abeyance for the duration of her marriage. Even then, however, the corporation sometimes gave permission for a woman married to a foreigner (non-free Englishman) to trade in the city, especially if she could have become free herself but for her marriage. In such cases, the woman, or her husband, petitioned the court of aldermen for permission to trade as a non-freeman, and the petitions are recorded in the repertories (i.e. proceedings) and papers of the court of aldermen in CLRO. There are manuscript subject (but not name) indexes to the repertories. In February 1694/5, for example, John Hunter's wife, Ann, who had become free herself some two years previously, before her marriage to him, was being 'obstructed in keeping a shop' in the city, as her freedom was technically in suspension, and John Hunter was a foreigner. They were obviously experiencing some hardship, for he petitioned, and she was allowed, to keep her shop 'without interruption ... especially because he was a great sufferer in the siege of Londonderry'.[4]

When searching for a female freeman, when a date of admission is not known, it is wise to check under both her maiden and married names, as she might have been admitted as an unmarried woman, or as a widow. The admission papers of a widow who was admitted by patrimony are useful in that they always give her father's, and thus her own maiden, name. However, they do not usually cite the deceased husband's name or details. For example, the admission papers in CLRO of Frances Ludlow record her as having been made free of the city by patrimony through the Grocers' Company in April 1804, she being 'Frances Ludlow, late Frances Ellis, daughter of Robert Ellis, Citizen and Grocer of London ... [he being] free ... 1759, ... [she having been born] 1766'.[5] However, the documents give no information at all about her late husband.

A widow of a city freeman could hold herself 'free by courtesy' under the custom of London after her husband's death. This allowed her to continue her late husband's business, and keep his apprentices without the trouble and expense of having to be formally admitted to the freedom herself. However, the very fact that she did not have to be admitted means that there are no records of such widows 'free by courtesy'.

In 1923, the rules forbidding the admission of married women were changed. Lady Parsons, a married woman, had applied to be admitted to the city freedom, and was initially refused, as the custom of London forbade the admission of married women. However, she persevered, pointing out that under the Sex Disqualification (Removal) Act, 1919, women were allowed to stand as local councillors, and that if she could not become a city freeman, she was effectively barred from standing as a common councilman for the city if she wished to do so. To comply with national law, the custom of London governing the city freedom was altered, and married women were admitted from 1923, the first two being Edie Anne Knight and Harriet Ann Sladen, who were both admitted on 20 April 1923. Lady Parsons herself was admitted on 26 July 1923. City freedom certificates and city freedom admission papers always give the marital status of married women being admitted between 1923 and 1987, since when the words 'married woman' have no longer been used on either types of document.

Interestingly, from 1924 the orphans of female, as well as male, freemen of the city were eligible for admission to the City of London Freemen's Orphan School (now the City of London Freemen's School) as foundation scholars (see section on rights and privileges in chapter 2 for further details), although freedom by patrimony through the mother as well as the father did not come into effect at that time. Admission to the freedom by patrimony was allowed to the children of female freemen on the same basis as for males only from 1976. For further details about this, see chapter 7.

Nationality

Until very recently, only British citizens (including subjects of the Empire and subsequently the Commonwealth) were normally admitted to the city freedom, as it involved an oath, and later a declaration, of allegiance to the British sovereign. This had to change, however, following legislation by the European Union (EU) permitting EU nationals to stand as local councillors, and to vote in elections, in any country within the EU. Rather than abolish the requirement for all common councilmen and aldermen to be city freemen, the regulations governing the admission of non-British subjects to the city freedom were adjusted from 1996. The vast majority of freemen admitted during the period covered by this book should have been British citizens, although, as we shall see, there were exceptions.

In the context of the freedom of the city of London, a non-British subject is referred to as an alien, whilst the word 'foreigner' almost always refers to a British non-freeman. In short, a foreigner came from another town, but an alien came from another country.

The technicalities of naturalisation can be complex, but suffice it to say that there was a difference, historically, between denization and naturalisation (although at various times, the city seems to have regarded both with suspicion). Denization was granted by royal letters patent, but was less comprehensive than naturalisation, which was granted by act of parliament, a much more expensive option. A denizen could purchase and devise land, but not inherit it, whereas a naturalised person could inherit it. Children born after their parents' denizations appear to have been considered subjects (except in the city), but those born before were only considered to be denizens. All the children of a naturalised person, whether born before or after the naturalisation, were considered native-born subjects. Naturalisation also involved swearing the oaths of allegiance and supremacy.

After 1844, naturalisation certificates began to be issued by the home secretary, and were enrolled on the close rolls 1844-73, which are held by the Public Record Office (PRO) in class C 54. Copies of naturalisation certificates are also held by the PRO in class HO 1 (covering 1844-1871) and HO 334 (covering 1870-1966). Subsequent records are held by the Home Office. Private naturalisation acts of parliament 1801-1947 are indexed in the official index to local and personal acts of parliament, whilst those who received naturalisation certificates 1844-1961 may be found in the indexes to the papers of the house of commons. Guildhall Library has copies of both indexes, as well as the Home Office's indexes to naturalisation certificates covering 1915-30. The PRO also has various indexes to naturalisations to 1961.

Aliens were admitted to the city freedom in the early middle ages, especially if they could assist London merchants to obtain similar trading advantages abroad, or were rich enough to be economically valuable to the city. They are recorded in the letter books, which record the proceedings of the courts of aldermen and of common council from 1275. Letter books A-L (1275-1498) have been edited by RR Sharpe, and published by the Corporation of London (see appendix 1). The admission of aliens at this period was regulated so as to ensure that they were respectable and trustworthy, and they had to find sureties for their good behaviour, but 'the object of these precautions was rather to keep out unsuitable characters than to hinder respectable foreigners becoming citizens of London.[6]

Later in the medieval period, especially after the economic crisis caused by the Black Death in the mid. 14th century, attitudes towards alien merchants became generally more restrictive in the face of commercial competition from merchants of other nations. In 1427, the court of common council ordered that no alien should be made a freeman of the city of London unless he was 'of the King's allegiance',[7] or naturalised. It was this order which was for centuries cited as the main stumbling-block to aliens being admitted to the city freedom, although there were many subsequent decisions which reflect the growing xenophobia of the 16th and 17th centuries. In particular, in 1574, an order was passed forbidding the children of aliens from being admitted to the city freedom, or being apprenticed to city freemen, even though 'the children of such strangers, being born within this realm, be by law accounted English'.[8] This order was not repealed until 1737, and even after that, its spirit lived on in the requirement that the sons of aliens had to petition to be allowed to become freemen.

Despite these orders, some alien freemen were admitted, usually because of influential royal patronage, or economic usefulness, although the corporation was not above refusing the king or queen's request on occasion. These admissions can be found in the journals (i.e. proceedings) of the court of common council in CLRO, which have subject, but not name, indexes, under the heading 'freedom'. In 1537, for example, at the request of the Lady Mary [the future Queen Mary I], the corporation agreed to the admission to the freedom of John Van De Antwarp, a goldsmith, and 'a very cunning [i.e. skilful] man', who had married an English woman.[9] Robert Thiery, silkweaver, recommended by the King, was allowed to be admitted in 1609, on account of his 'extraordinary skill and invention in making stuff of silkworms nourished in England'.[10]

During the period of the Huguenot immigration, from the 1680s into the early 18th century, considerable numbers of French Protestant refugees arrived in this country and formed a useful addition to the economy, forming, for example, the well-known colony of weavers in Spitalfields. At the same time, numbers of Dutch immigrants were also arriving with the advent of the Dutch William of Orange, who became King William III of England (1689-1702). During this period, a number of general naturalisation acts of parliament were passed, allowing alien Protestants in particular trades to become naturalised subjects of this country under certain conditions [e.g. acts of 1663 (15 Chas II, cap. 15); 1708 (7 Anne, cap. 5) repealed in 1711 (10 Anne, cap. 5); 1749 (13 Geo II, cap. 7), etc.]. The Huguenot Society has published naturalisations and denizations between 1509 and 1800, and these publications are listed in appendix 1.

Attempts at passing general naturalisation acts of parliament were also made in 1672-73 and 1693, although these were defeated, and were opposed by the Corporation of London, largely on the grounds that the city would lose revenues gathered from the package and scavage dues, payable on aliens' goods coming into the city. Another attempt was made in 1747, which again the city corporation opposed.[11]

It appears that, from the journals of the court of common council, the only freemen who might be said to be remotely alien and who were being admitted after about 1700 were the sons of aliens who had been naturalised or who had received letters of denization, and they always had to petition the court of common council to be allowed to be admitted by redemption, even if they were applying through a city livery company. Some of these petitions, which are usually to be found in the freedom admission papers in CLRO, can be quite detailed, supplying valuable information about the country of origin of the applicant's parents, when they came to this country, and what their business was. By the beginning of the 19th century, the petitions become briefer and more formulaic, but still provide some useful information. For example, John Benjamin Tolkien's petition, approved by the court of common council on 22 April 1813 states that he was 'the son of John Benjamin Tolkien a native of Dantzic [now Gdansk, Poland] who came to England about the year 1752 when he married a native of this country and has resided here ever since, and where your petitioner was born'.[12] The same year saw petitions allowed from the sons of aliens from all over Europe, for example Peter Augustus Stocqueler, son of Joseph Christian Stocqueler, deceased, who had come to England in 1773 from Lisbon, Portugal; Lewis de Beaune, son of David Henry de Beaune, who had arrived from Yverdon, Switzerland in 1770 and William George Rolfes, son of Frederick Rolfes who arrived from Hanover about 50 years before.[13] The requirement for the sons of aliens to petition for admission appears to continue in the common council minutes until 1855, but no later ones are found. The petitions are briefly minuted in the common council minutes after 1811 (annually subject indexed), as well as written out in full in the more detailed journals of the court of common council (cumulatively subject indexed), and the originals are preserved in the common council papers, with copies filed in the city freedom admission papers in CLRO.

During the First World War, when anti-German feelings were running high, the Corporation of London passed certain orders designed to prevent Germans, or former Germans, from becoming city freemen. On 18 May 1916, the court of common council ruled that 'no German, naturalised or otherwise, be permitted to take up the freedom of the city either by apprenticeship or redemption until otherwise ordered by this court'.[14] As a corollary of this measure, on 24 January 1918 the city chamberlain was instructed to include on city freedom application forms a question as to whether the applicant was naturalised, and when, and whether their original nationality had been given up. If the applicant had changed his name, this also had to be disclosed on the application form, which usually survives amongst the city freedom admission papers in CLRO. Whilst the motives for introducing these measures might seem reprehensible today, the genealogist can only be thankful for them, as they ensure that valuable information is supplied, particularly as many people with German-sounding names changed them around the time of the First World War. Widening xenophobia at that time also led to the court of common council ordering, on 8 February 1917, that the city freedom should not be 'granted to any person who is a subject of any country which is now at war with this country, or at the time of the application shall be at war with this country, or who has not renounced for all purposes his original citizenship ... and has further proved that he has acquired a British domicile'.[15] The requirement for the date of naturalisation to appear on application papers, and the bans on former German subjects, or former subjects of countries at war with Britain, were repealed on 30 April 1953.[16]

Race and religion

Although considered abhorrent and illegal today, racial discrimination was a sad, and legal, fact throughout much of this country's history, and the admission of black people to the city freedom was officially banned by the court of aldermen in 1731. However, it is not known how many black people might have been admitted before that date, or when they began to be admitted again after it. It is certainly true that despite other bans, aliens were admitted after being banned in 1427, and Jewish freemen were certainly being admitted for a period before 1738, although they were not formally allowed to be free before 1830 (see previous section and below).

The case, in 1731, which led to the ban on black people becoming free was that of John Satia, who was apprenticed to William Attey, Citizen and Joiner of London, on 11 March 1717/18. Satia served his full term, and thus completed the criteria for admission by servitude (servitude is the technical term for admission by apprenticeship: the word in the context of the city freedom has no connotation of slavery, and indeed there is no evidence in the corporation's archives to suppose that Satia had been a slave). Under the custom of London, admission to the city freedom by servitude after fulfilling the criteria was a right, not a privilege, and could not be refused, but despite this, Satia's path to becoming a city freeman was anything but smooth. He had to petition to secure his admission, stating that he had 'often heard Mr Gerrard, a merchant since deceased, say that he brought him from Barbados when he was about two years old, and that he was born there, and that the said Mr Gerrard put him out as an apprentice'. The chamberlain sought clarification as to admitting him, ostensibly on the grounds that there was no documentary proof that he was a British subject, and not an alien, but the court of aldermen, whilst allowing Satia to become free, subsequently ordered that in future no black person should be bound apprentice or made a freeman of any of the city livery companies, thus effectively barring them from the city freedom also.[17]

Before 1830, the freeman's oath had to be sworn on the Bible, and this effectively prevented non-Christians from becoming city freemen. It also presented an obstacle to the admission of some members of some Christian denominations, such as Quakers, from becoming city freemen, although in the case of the Quakers this was overcome after 1696.

Members of the Society of Friends (Quakers) did not have to swear the oath after 4 May 1696, when the Affirmation Act 1696 [7 & 8 William III, cap. 34] took effect. Under this act, Quakers could affirm instead of taking oaths for most legal purposes. However, the legality of Quakers affirming instead of taking the freeman's oath was clearly still rather a grey area in 1713, when the Corporation of London asked for counsel's opinion on the subject. The case presented for opinion is interesting because it tells us exactly what happened at that time when a Quaker was admitted to the city freedom: 'of late the method hath been that when a Quaker is to be admitted into the freedom, instead of taking either oath or affirmation, the oath of a freeman is read in their hearing and they are asked in the words following, viz. You declare in the presence of Almighty God that you consent to all the articles contained in that oath, who answers, yea, and subscribes their names to the annext paper and thereupon they are entred in the book of freedoms'.[18] In other words, the Quaker listened to the oath being read and was asked if he or she agreed to the tenets of it. If they answered 'yes', they then signed some kind of a document (not present in the archives today, alas) and their names were admitted into the freedom book. The city freedom admission papers of Quakers were usually marked with a 'Q' from 1696 onwards.

Jewish and other non-Christian British subjects were allowed to be admitted to the city freedom after 1830, although they appear to have been admitted for a period before 1738 without specific permission being seen to be necessary. As stated in the previous section, there were failed attempts at passing general naturalisation acts of parliament made in the late 17th and 18th centuries which were opposed by the Corporation of London, because the city would lose package and scavage dues from aliens' goods coming into the city. The city's tenant collector of the package and scavage dues, Richard Pierce, was keen to prove that he would lose money if a General Naturalisation Act were passed, and, in compiling evidence for his case, he made lists covering the period of about 1680s-1700 of aliens who had obtained naturalisation or denization, and those of them (about twenty persons) who had also obtained the freedom of the city of London. These lists are held by CLRO.[19] One of these lists is particularly interesting, as it notes several Jewish naturalised freemen: it is otherwise the case that Jewish freemen were not admissible to the city freedom until 1830. No-one seems to have been particularly concerned about Jewish freemen until 1738, when one Abraham Rathorn was refused admission, although his father, Isaac, had been a city freeman and a freeman of the Loriners' Company. Abraham brought a writ of *mandamus* against the chamberlain, insisting that he be admitted, but although the city solicitor was instructed to defend the action, the result does not appear in the city's records. Shortly afterwards, a Committee was set up to enquire by what means Jewish freemen had been admitted, and to bring in a Bill to prevent it if necessary. However, once again, the Committee's findings do not appear in the city's records.[20]

On 10 December 1830, the court of common council passed an act 'for enabling all persons born within this Kingdom, and all natural born subjects whatsoever, not professing the Christian religion, but in other respects qualified, to be admitted to the freedom of the city of London, upon taking the freeman's oath, according to the forms of their own religion'.[21] Joseph Lewis was the first Jewish freeman of the city of London to be so admitted after the 1830 act, by servitude (i.e. apprenticeship) through the Coopers' Company on 1 February 1831, according to an annotation in the freedom book in CLRO: 'This person is the first British born subject not professing the Christian religion admitted under the act of common council of the 10th December 1830'.[22] Subsequent Jewish freemen have their entries in the freedom book annotated 'sworn on the Pentateuch'.

This 1830 act of common council is commonly held to be an example of the Corporation of London's early liberal views, particularly with regard to Jewish emancipation. However, immediately after the admission of Joseph Lewis the court of aldermen, acting in defiance of common council, blocked the admission of Jewish applicants for the city freedom by redemption (who were admitted by discretion, whereas Joseph Lewis had been free by servitude, to which he had a right, and which they had no discretion to block). There was clearly some friction between the courts of aldermen and common council over the issue, but the court of common council won, and from June 1831 Jewish applicants for admission by redemption were admitted on the same basis as other applicants by common council and the court of aldermen alike.

Many Jewish applicants were themselves naturalised aliens, or the children of aliens, and therefore had to petition the court of common council for permission to be admitted. Once again, these petitions, minuted in the common council minutes, with the original petitions usually in the common council papers, can be very informative about applicants and their family origins.

Admission and the freeman's oath or declaration

There are four ways of becoming a freeman, and a person can be admitted:

1. as an honorary freeman;
2. by servitude;
3. by patrimony; or
4. by redemption.

Each of these means of admission can be undertaken either through, or without, the intervention of one of the livery companies (although before 1835, one *had* to be a livery company member first). Chapters 5-8 take each of these types of admission in turn, and describe the documents which record each, and the information contained in them.

All admissions (except for a few individual honorary ones) took place in the chamberlain's court in Guildhall. It was up to the intending freeman to make sure that he had gathered together all the necessary proofs and documents to ensure that he qualified for the freedom.

A person being admitted by servitude needed to have his master, or another person, often from his livery company, to swear that he had completed his service. Otherwise the master could provide a written certificate, and these are often filed with the apprenticeship indenture in the city freedom admission papers in CLRO, especially from the 19th century.

A person being admitted by patrimony needed to be able to prove, either with six guarantors, also known as vouchers or compurgators, or by producing certificates, that he was the legal and natural son of his father, and that his father was a freeman before he was born. This usually entailed producing to the clerk his father's 'copy' (freedom certificate), although this is not filed in the admission papers: the clerk merely copied the salient details of the father's freedom onto the intending freeman's admission papers. After 1837, the freeman might well have had to show the clerk his birth certificate (since the later 19th century this has been obligatory), but the certificates are never retained in the admission papers.

Candidates for admission by redemption had to bring the copy of the order of the court of aldermen or common council allowing their admission, and this copy order is usually filed in the freedom admission papers. The date at the top of this order is always the date of the meeting of the court of aldermen or common council which allowed their admission: it is not necessarily the date of their actual admission. See chapter 8 for further details of admissions by redemption.

The applicant then usually came to the chamberlain's court for admission, where the clerk of the chamberlain's court (or clerk of the chamber, in earlier times) administered the freeman's oath. This was sworn on the bible only until 1830, after which time it could be sworn according to the forms of other religions (e.g. on the Pentateuch for Jewish freemen). Quakers could affirm after 1696. The oath became a declaration by an act of parliament of 1849 (12 & 13 Vict, cap. 94, para. 10), and barring a few changes recently, it is fundamentally the same as the oath which was sworn by freemen in the middle ages. The freeman's declaration laid down by the 1849 Act is as follows:

> 'I [name] do solemnly declare that I will be good and true to our sovereign [lady Queen Victoria]; that I will be obedient to the mayor of this city; that I will maintain the franchises and customs thereof, and will keep this city harmless in that which in me is; that I will keep the [Queen]'s peace in my own person; that I will know no gatherings or conspiracies made against the [Queen]'s peace, but I will warn the mayor thereof, or hinder it to my power; and that all these points and articles I will well and truly keep according to the laws and customs of this city, to my power'.[23]

On admission, the new freeman has for many years been presented with a little book, bound in red, called *Rules for the conduct of life*. Little is known of the history of this little book, but the earliest existing book of that title is held by Guildhall Library, with a publication date of about 1770, although a watermark places it at about 1802. Details of similar uplifting works and pious advice to apprentices are given in chapter 6.

4

ARCHIVES RELATING TO THE CITY FREEDOM

Records of city freedom admissions before 1681

Few records survive for the admission of freemen of the city of London before 1681, owing to a fire at Guildhall in 1786, which destroyed many records then kept in the chamberlain's strongroom. What records exist are usually of very limited use to the family historian, as they tend to give only the freeman's name, livery company and date of admission.

1309-1312

City freemen admitted between 1309 and 1312 are recorded in letter book D at CLRO. The letter books record the proceedings of the courts of common council and of aldermen from 1275, and the letter books 1275-1498 have been edited and published (see appendix 1 for details). Letter book D (1309-1314) contains a transcript of part of a register of freemen, and it is published and indexed in RR Sharpe, *Calendar of letter book D* (Corporation of London, 1902).

1437-1497

Recognizance rolls 13-25 in CLRO record freemen admitted by redemption only between 1437 and 1497, together with their sureties, and there is a card index also in CLRO.

1495-1649

The same card index in CLRO indexes freemen admitted by redemption only between 1495 and 1649. Because admissions by redemption were discretionary, permission had to be given by the court of aldermen, and so the names of freemen requesting admission by redemption appear in the repertories (i.e. proceedings) of the court of aldermen in CLRO. At the time in question, probably only about 10% of city freemen were admitted by redemption, and so the index is far from comprehensive.

c.1551-1553

For the period around 1551-53, fragments of two registers of freemen survive. One is held by CLRO,[24] but the other is in the British Library.[25] Both are published in

Charles Welch, *Register of freemen of the city of London ...*, (London and Middlesex Archaeological Society, 1908). However, the published edition contains some errors, and corrections appear in 'A London manuscript' by Bower Marsh in *The Genealogist*, New Series XXXII, Apr 1916, pp 217-220.

1668-1669

CLRO has a register of freemen 1668-69, which was badly burnt in a fire in Guildhall in 1786. It has since been conserved, and a full typed transcript (which is complete, and much easier to use than the original, even after conservation) is held by CLRO, as is a card index.

Records of city freedom admissions after 1681

1681-1940

The city freedom archives in CLRO form a large collection, and certainly not all of them are useful to the family historian. There is a list of the most useful series at appendix 3. The single most useful series, however, is the monthly bundles of city freedom admission papers 1681-1940 (over 2,800 bundles). Whilst there are a few gaps in the series, most notably around the 1680s and 1770s to 1780s, they are remarkably complete. City freedom admission papers after 1940 are still held in the Chamberlain's Court in Guildhall, where admissions to the city freedom still take place.

The admission papers are indexed in a series of large volumes of 'alphabets', each volume covering a group of years. These alphabets can be time-consuming to search, so it helps if a date of birth (a city freeman could only be admitted after the age of 21) or freedom admission (perhaps from a certificate, or other source) is known. The alphabets contain the names of all freemen admitted for the period covered by the volume. Within that period, the book is divided into sections for each letter of the alphabet, and all the surnames for each initial letter are then entered in date order. The only information in the alphabets (which some people incorrectly call the 'freedom registers') is the freeman's name, livery company (not necessarily the same as their occupation), month of admission (not actual day) and how admitted (honorary, servitude, patrimony or redemption). These means of admission are abbreviated in the alphabets to:

Hon'y	honorary
S	servitude (apprenticeship to a city freeman)
S (not inrolled)	servitude (but the apprenticeship was not enrolled in the chamberlain's court, and a higher fee for the freedom admission is therefore payable)
P	patrimony
R	redemption (purchase)
RCA	redemption, court of aldermen (i.e. through a livery company)
RCC	redemption, court of common council (i.e. not through a livery company, possible only after October 1835)
PR	redemption, due to the person being on the register of parliamentary electors for the city of London (possible only from October 1856)

These terms are explained more fully in later chapters. When searching the alphabets, it pays to note down the information from all these headings, as well as the call numbers for ordering the bundles. The documents in the monthly bundles of admission papers take different forms, depending on the type of admission. If you know from the alphabet that a freeman was free by servitude ('S'), then you can look in the bundle for the typical apprenticeship indenture, for example. Patrimony and redemption papers are each also distinguishable, and so when looking through a monthly bundle of up to two hundred admissions for your one person's admission papers, you can safely ignore those documents which you know relate to other sorts of admission. The different types of document are described more fully later on in the book, and illustrated (see Plates III-IX).

The information given in the monthly bundles of admission papers also depends on the date. On the whole, you can usually expect to find the freeman's name and livery company, and his or her father's name, abode and occupation or livery company, although there is a period around and just after 1800 when the father's details were totally omitted by the recording clerks from redemption admissions (see chapter 8 for details). Freemen's occupations and addresses usually only appear after 1835, when an application form began to be used for applicants for the freedom by redemption. Dates of birth usually only appear when the freeman is admitted by patrimony, or in late 19th and 20th century admission papers.

On very rare occasions, the admission papers contain records which are not actually admission papers, or records of translations between livery companies, at all.

Sometimes, for example, such records merely correct a misspelt surname, written by a clerk for an illiterate freeman, and not noticed, perhaps, until the freeman's son turned up to obtain the city freedom by patrimony many years later with an ostensibly different name. The bundle of city freedom admission papers for August 1719, for example, contains two documents headed 'no freedom, only to be put on ye file of Aug 1719'. On closer inspection, these turn out to be a petition to the court of aldermen presented on 10 February 1718/9, and a certificate of the Barber Surgeons' Company dated 29 July 1719. The certificate records that the freedom admission register of the Barber Surgeons' Company had been altered, in accordance with an order of the court of aldermen of 30 June 1719, to add the words '(*alias* Benson)' after the entry for the company freedom admission of Thomas Piggott. But more interesting is the petition to the court of aldermen which prompted the order in the first place:

> '... the humble representation and petition of Thomas Benson, setting forth that his father dying while he was young, his uncle and guardian bred him in the country and cheated him of his name and estate, and bound him apprentice to one Saltmarsh by the name of Thomas Piggott, and by that name the petitioner was free, although his true name is Thomas Benson, and praying that his right name may be entered in the chamberlain's books instead of that of Piggott'.[26]

The 'chamberlain's books' of city freedom admissions do not survive before 1784, but luckily, the chamberlain's clerks filed the copy petition in the city freedom admission papers, and thus a little more information survives than a mere '(*alias* Benson)'.

1784 to date

CLRO also holds freedom books (*alias* registers, or declaration books, or the 'chamberlain's books') 1784 to date. These give no more personal information about freemen than the admission papers, but do give the exact day of admission, often not given in the admission papers. These freedom books were originally identified by letters, and are referred to in freedom certificates and patrimony papers as 'the book marked with the letter T' for example. Many of the early freedom books were rebound in the 19th century, and the original letters were not put back on to the new spines. However, CLRO has a list of the known letters, and to which volumes they apply.

These two series are the chief source for city freedom admissions 1681-1940. They are usually complemented by the records of the city livery companies, which include records of apprentices bound by the companies and of company freemen admitted.

Sometimes, the company records will give an address which has been omitted from a city freedom admission document, or a particular company clerk might supply additional personal information for a particular period. More importantly, the gaps in the city freedom admission papers (most notably around the 1680s and 1770s to 1780s) can sometimes be filled by livery company records. Most city livery company records are held by the Manuscripts Section of Guildhall Library, but a few are still held by the relevant company. A list of the city livery companies, and the whereabouts of their records, is given in appendix 2. Some companies' apprenticeship bindings have been published and indexed by Cliff Webb for the Society of Genealogists, and a list of these publications to date appears in appendix 1.

Because they are the best set of records, this book will refer mainly to the city freedom admission papers in CLRO. Perhaps the best way to describe the types of document to be found, and the information in them, is to look at each of the ways in which a city freeman can, or could, be admitted, and to describe the records relevant to each.

5
THE HONORARY FREEDOM

Honorary freemen are usually very distinguished or otherwise worthy people, and there are comparatively few of them.

Individual admissions

A person who receives the honorary freedom of the city of London receives the highest honour the Corporation of London can bestow, and this does not happen very often. When the corporation wishes to honour someone in this way, a special resolution is passed by the court of common council (see plate III for an example). After the resolution has been passed, the recipient is invited to a special ceremony at Guildhall, where the chamberlain of London formally admits him or her to the freedom. A formal entertainment usually follows, either at Guildhall itself, or at the Mansion House, the lord mayor's official residence, or both. Admission to the honorary freedom is always a grand affair, and the speeches made by the chamberlain and by the individual recipients of the honorary freedom at their admissions between 1757 and 1959 are published in *London's roll of fame 1757-1884* and *London's roll of fame 1885-1959* (Corporation of London, 1884 and 1959 respectively). A full list of individual grants of the honorary city freedom appears at appendix 4.

From 1792, a beautifully coloured and illuminated copy of the resolution to admit the honorary freeman was presented to him or her on admission, and duplicates of these were made until 1856 and kept by the chamberlain's court. Over eighty of them are now in CLRO.

Group admissions

Before the end of the 19th century, all honorary freemen were admitted as individuals (e.g. Nelson), but during the 20th century, in addition to such individual honorary admissions, all of the qualifying members of particular groups have been admitted. These group admissions comprise:

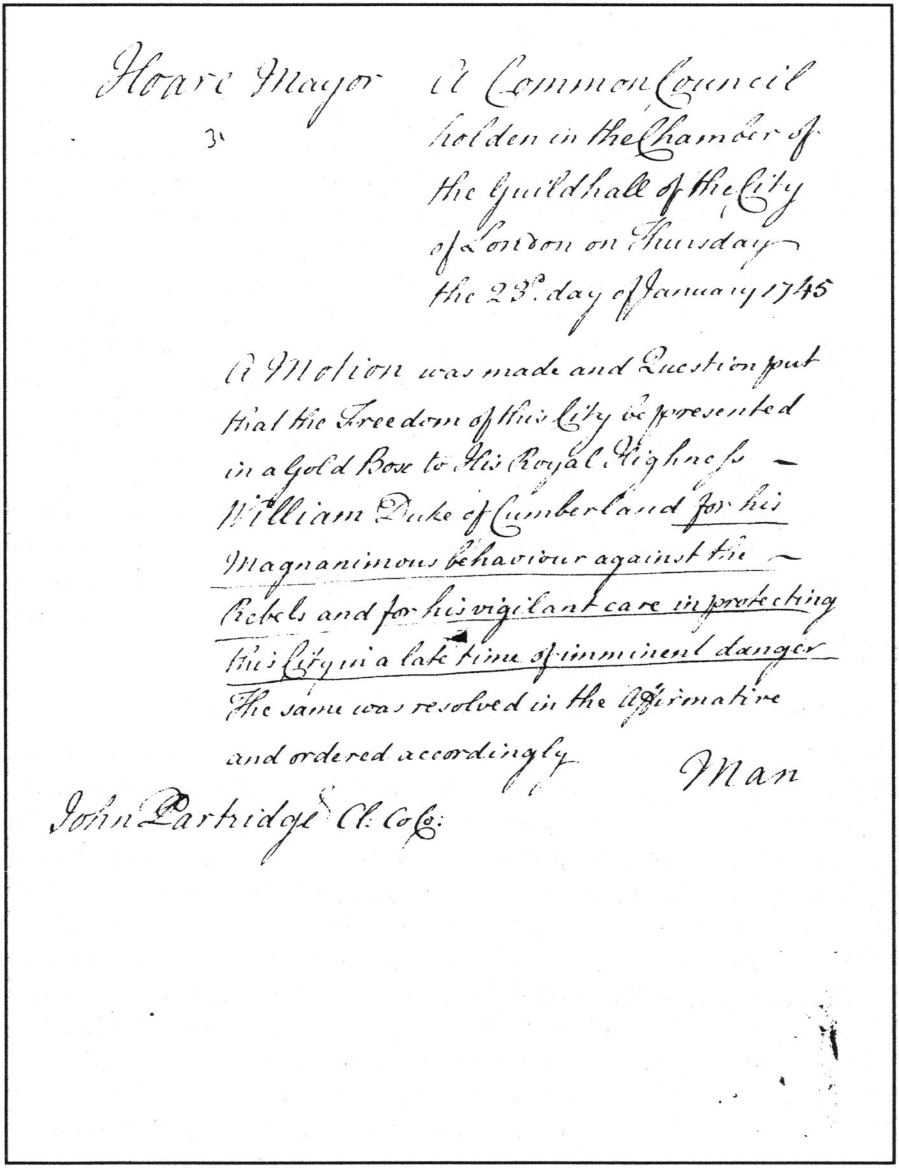

Hoare Mayor

3º

It Common Council
holden in the Chamber of
the Guildhall of the City
of London on Thursday
the 23º. day of January 1745

A Motion was made and Question put
that the Freedom of this City be presented
in a Gold Box to His Royal Highness —
William Duke of Cumberland for his
Magnanimous behaviour against the —
Rebels and for his vigilant care in protecting
this City in a late time of imminent danger
The same was resolved in the Affirmative
and ordered accordingly

Man

John Partridge Cl. Coñ:

Plate III: Common Council Order, 23 January 1745/6, for the Honorary Freedom to be Granted to HRH William, Duke of Cumberland (Free August 1746) [CLRO reference: CF1/697/1a]

City Imperial Volunteers (CIVs)

Members of the City Imperial Volunteer (CIV) force, which fought in the Boer War, were ordered to be admitted to the honorary city freedom by the court of common council on 20 December 1899.[27] The CIV force of 1,600 men was organised with remarkable speed, under the direction of the Lord Mayor, Sir Alfred Newton, in December 1899. The first batch of 500 CIV honorary city freedom admissions took place in Guildhall on 12 January 1900, and the men departed for Southampton for embarkation the next day. Most of the rest of the CIV admissions and embarkations took place in or around January 1900. The CIVs were back in England and disbanded by 31 October 1900. There is a full list of members of the CIV force in the published *Reports on the raising, organising, equipping and despatching the City of London Imperial Volunteers to South Africa*, published by order of the Rt. Hon. the Lord Mayor, Sir Alfred J Newton, Bart. (London, June 1900).[28] Amongst the city freedom admission archives, CLRO has only freedom declaration books, which contain the CIV men's signatures at the foot of the freeman's declaration, and a bundle of papers which contains the names, and sometimes the addresses, of some of their next of kin. However, CLRO does hold some surviving CIV archives (some of the more useful of which are listed in appendix 3), as does Guildhall Library.

First World War: sons of members of the court of common council

The grant of the honorary freedom to sons of members of the court of common council who fought in HM Forces in the First World War was ordered by the court of common council on 19 September 1918.[29] Admissions were to commence after the end of the war, and their names were to be inscribed on a tablet in Guildhall. A roll of honour was also to be placed in Guildhall, containing the names of all those members and their sons who had been killed in the War. Rather interestingly, in 1920, two common councilmen proposed that the honorary freedom should be extended to include the daughters of members of the court of common council who had served in the Forces during the War. However, this proposal was rejected on the grounds that 'the services rendered do not appear to be of such a nature as to entitle any of the ladies to the honour proposed'.[30] It was therefore only the surviving sons of members who were admitted in the ceremony at Guildhall on 10 December 1920.[31] 82 were admitted on that day, 7 more between then and 21 April 1921, and 4 were then still entitled to receive it, but were still abroad. Certificates of thanks were given to those who were already freemen, 14 of which had been issued by 21 April 1921, with 7 more still waiting to be awarded at that date.[32] A full list of all 114 of these sons of members (but not their dates of admission), and a list of the names appearing on the memorial to those killed, is held by CLRO.[33]

First World War: city police reserve

On 3 June 1920, the court of common council ordered that the honorary freedom be presented to all special constables who were not already city freemen, and who had joined the special police reserve in 1914 and were still serving on 3 June 1920.[34] In addition, 'suitable certificates' were to be awarded to all men who had completed three years' efficient service. The five hundred or so men who had served all through the War and were still serving were admitted at a ceremony at Guildhall on 26 October 1920, whilst the '3-year men' had their certificates posted to them privately.[35] CLRO has no separate list of either of these groups of men and the freedom book signed by those admitted to the freedom on admission is so badly charred, probably following the burning of Guildhall in December 1940, that it cannot be handled. However, the names of those made free appear in the alphabets of freedom admissions, and the admission papers have survived.

First World War: former pupils of Corporation of London schools

Former pupils of the Corporation of London's schools who fought in the First World War were admitted in accordance with an order of the court of common council of 20 May 1915, by which the city freedom was to be granted 'free of cost, upon all officers and men serving with HM naval and military forces, who have been students in any of the corporation Schools, and who intimate their desire to accept the same'. An amendment that all members of the city police force who were serving with the forces should also be awarded the honorary freedom was turned down, however.[36] Men given the honorary freedom under this order were admitted individually from May 1915 until after the war ended, and their names appear in the alphabets of freedom admissions. Individual admission papers in CLRO for these men comprise three forms. Form A is an application form, and usually contains the freeman's name, address, date and place of birth, and present rank and basic service details (e.g. regiment), plus his father's name. Form B certifies the freeman's qualifying attendance at the particular corporation School, and form C certifies his service in the forces.

Obviously, these papers will lead the researcher on to the records of the appropriate Corporation of London school, which at that time would have been the City of London School, the City of London Freemen's Orphan School [the word 'orphan' was dropped from the title in 1926] or the Guildhall School of Music [now the

Guildhall School of Music and Drama]. Many of the surviving pupil records for these schools are held by CLRO, and these are detailed in appendix 3. They include full records of pupils of the City of London School 1837-1900 and of the City of London Freemen's Orphan School 1853-1955 (75 year closure period). More recent records than these are believed to be still at the respective schools. Records of the Guildhall School of Music are in CLRO up to the 1980s, although they are not believed to be complete, particularly for the period before the First World War. They can be supplemented to some degree by the lists of prizewinners which are printed in the early prospectuses, or the press cuttings scrapbooks, which are also in CLRO. There are also published histories of most of the corporation's schools, which are listed in appendix 1.

Second World War: city fire guard commanders

Following an order of the court of common council of 12 July 1945, the 400 or so sector and block commanders of the city fire guard who were not already freemen were 'invited to take up the freedom and be admitted without payment of fee'.[37] They were also given individual resolutions of thanks. Each man was individually admitted, with most admissions being in or shortly after September and October 1945. The city freedom admission papers for each man usually state the name, address, date and place of birth of the freeman, plus the name and address of his father. Because they were admitted after 1940, the city freedom admission papers for the city fire guard commanders are still in the custody of the chamberlain's court at Guildhall.

6

ADMISSION BY SERVITUDE (APPRENTICESHIP TO A CITY FREEMAN)

In order to be admitted to the city freedom by servitude, a person had to complete an apprenticeship to a city freeman, almost always described as a 'Citizen and [something] of London' (or, after 1835, possibly just 'Citizen of London'). Under an act of common council of 1574, the apprentice could not be the child of an alien (a non-British subject). 'Servitude' might have derogatory connotations elsewhere but, in a city of London context, it is the correct term for admission to the freedom both of the city and of the city livery companies by completion of a full term of apprenticeship to a master who was a city freeman.

Provided that all the requirements had been fulfilled, the courts of aldermen and common council had no discretion to veto an application for admission by servitude. However, if the terms of the apprenticeship indenture had been broken (e.g. if the apprentice had married during the term of the apprenticeship), the apprentice had to petition the court of aldermen (or the court of common council, after 1835, if he were not apprenticed through a city company) to be allowed to become free, and it was up to the relevant court whether they allowed this by servitude or not. If admission by servitude was not allowed in such cases, the apprentice could be admitted by redemption (purchase) at the discretion of the particular court. It is common in such cases for the city freedom admission papers in CLRO to contain a copy of the applicant's petition, which usually outlines the terms of the original apprenticeship, and states how the contract had been broken. Sometimes the original apprenticeship indenture also survives, pinned to the petition, either in the freedom admission papers or in the papers of the court of aldermen or common council for the date on which the petition was heard.

Apprenticeship in the city of London

Before 1889, city of London apprenticeships had to last for a minimum of 7 years, and this was the normal term, although a few apprenticeship indentures amongst the city freedom admission papers show terms of 8 or 9 years, or, very rarely, longer. In 1889, the minimum term of apprenticeship was shortened to 4 years, although even after that date, the traditional 7-year term remained common.

Within the city of London, the apprentice, even though under the age of 21, and therefore technically a minor, could sign his or her own apprenticeship indenture, which was considered a legally binding document.

Most (before 1835, all) apprenticeships were to city freemen who were also freemen of one of the city companies. Records of apprentice bindings often survive amongst the relevant company archives in the Manuscripts Section of Guildhall Library, and the bindings of an increasing number of companies have been extracted by Cliff Webb and published by the Society of Genealogists (see appendix 1 for a list of these).

The next stage in the proceedings was that, within one year of the apprenticeship beginning, the master enrolled it in the chamberlain's court. If this did not occur (as happened quite often), it could not be done later, and the apprentice had to pay a higher fee if and when he finally obtained his city freedom. Not enrolling the apprenticeship could give the apprentice grounds to 'sue out his indentures' in the mayor's court, thus cancelling the apprenticeship, although in such cases, the apprentice might have had other grievances too. In many cases, the masters probably either forgot, or were unwilling to pay the inevitable fee.

Records of apprentice bindings and of enrolment can be useful for the genealogist if the ancestor sought did not eventually become a freeman of the company or city. Many factors could lead to an apprenticeship not being completed, in the city as elsewhere. Not all apprentices who were bound apprentice to a city or company freeman, or who enrolled their apprenticeships within the first year went on to complete them, or to become company or city freemen. It also follows that not all persons who eventually became free by servitude necessarily had their apprentice-ships enrolled in the first place, although these apprenticeships should have been recorded by their company.

Records of apprenticeship enrolments in the chamber of London survive only after 1786, and comprise the 'inrolment books' [sic] 1786-1974 (16 volumes, 1913-40 on microfilm only), indexed in alphabets (9 volumes) similar to the freedom admission alphabets. These records are held at CLRO and more recent records have a 30 year closure period. There is little point in checking the inrolment books for people who were admitted as city freemen, as the entries in the inrolment books merely repeat the information to be found on the apprenticeship indenture usually filed in the admission papers: they usually note the apprentice's name, his or her father's name, abode and occupation, the master's name and city company, and the commencement date and length of the apprenticeship. The alphabets of apprenticeship inrolments can be as lengthy as the city freedom admission alphabets to search, but can be worthwhile if the apprentice never became a freeman.

The form of apprenticeship indentures in the city of London

The usual document to be found in the city freedom admission papers for freemen by servitude is the freeman's apprenticeship indenture (see plate IV for an example). Although apprenticeship was a private contract, apprenticeships to city freemen were governed by long usage and the custom of London, which laid down a standard form for the indenture. The wording before 1 May 1710 was usually as follows (words in square brackets indicate individual manuscript additions to the standard printed form: note that this particular apprenticeship was, unusually, for 8 years):

'This indenture witnesseth that [John Adams, son of William Adams late of East Hardwick in the County of York gent. deceased] doth put himself apprentice to [William Pott] Citizen and [Apothecary] of London, to learn his art; and with him, after the manner of an apprentice, to serve from the [first day of May last past], unto the full end and term of [eight] years, from thence next following, to be fully complete and ended. During which term, the said apprentice his said master faithfully shall serve, his secrets keep, his lawful commands every where gladly do. He shall do no damage to his said master, nor see to be done of others; but that he to his power shall let, or forthwith give warning to his said master of the same. He shall not commit fornication, nor contract matrimony, within the said term. He shall not play at cards, dice, tables, or any other unlawful games, whereby his said master may have any loss. With his own goods or others, during the said term, without licence of his said master, he shall neither buy nor sell. He shall not haunt taverns or play-houses, nor absent himself from his said master's service day or night unlawfully. But in all things as a faithful apprentice he shall behave himself towards his said master, and all his, during the said term. And the said master his said apprentice in the same art and mystery which he useth, by the best means that he can, shall teach and instruct, or cause to be taught and instructed; finding to his said apprentice, meat, drink, apparel, lodging and all other necessaries, according to the custom of the city of London, during the said term. And, for the true performance of all and every the said covenants and agreements, either of the said parties bindeth himself unto the other by these presents. In witness whereof the parties above-named to these indentures interchangeably have put their hands and seals the [fifth] day of [June] Anno Dom. 16[83] and in the [xxxvth] year of our sovereign Lord King Charles the II'.[38]

From 1 May 1710 until 1811, a stamp duty was payable on the premiums paid for all apprenticeships throughout Great Britain, except for those paid for by charities or

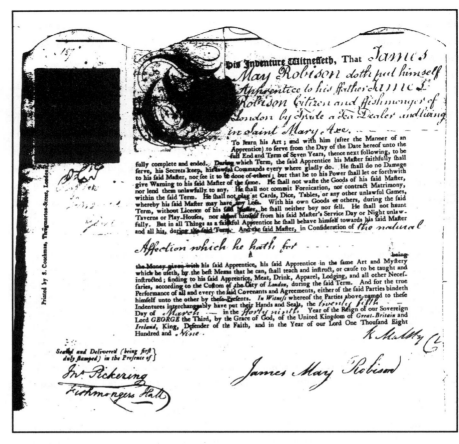

Plate VI: Typical Pre-1719 Patrimony Paper of Joseph Webb, Free June 1691 [CLRO reference: ELJL/47/99]

parishes, and so after 1710, a space is left on the standard printed city indenture form which is filled in with the amount paid, thus:

'This indenture witnesseth that [Richard Fauston son of James Fauston of Peckham in the County of Middlesex [*sic*] Cordwainer] doth put himself apprentice to [James Hopwood] Citizen and [Girdler] of London, to learn his art; and with him, after the manner of an apprentice, to serve from the day of the date hereof, until the full end and term of [seven] years, from thence next following, to be fully complete and ended. During which term, the said apprentice his said master faithfully shall serve, his secrets keep, his lawful commands every where gladly do. He shall do no damage to his said master, nor see it to be done of others; but that he to the utmost of his power shall let, or forthwith give warning to his said master of the same. He shall not waste the goods of his said master, nor lend them unlawfully to any. He shall not commit fornication, nor contract matrimony, within the said term. He shall not play at cards, dice, tables, or any other unlawful games, whereby his said master may have any loss. With his own goods or others, during the said term, without licence of his said master, he shall neither buy nor sell. He shall not haunt taverns or play-houses, nor absent himself from his said master's service day or night unlawfully. But in all things as a faithfull apprentice he shall behave himself towards his said master, and all his, during the said term. And the said master, in consideration of [five shillings of good and lawful money of the United Kingdom of Great Britain and Ireland, current in England] being the money given with his said apprentice, his said apprentice in the same art and mystery which he useth, by the best means that he can, shall teach and instruct, or cause to be taught and instructed; finding to his said apprentice, meat, drink, apparel, lodging and all other necessaries, according to the custom of the city of London, during the said term.
And, for the true performance of all and every the said covenants and agreements, either of the said parties bindeth himself unto the other by these presents. In witness whereof the parties above-named to these indentures interchangeably have put their hands and seals the [sixth] day of [October] in the [forty-seventh] year of the reign our sovereign Lord George III of the United Kingdom of Great Britain and Ireland, King, Defender of the Faith, and in the year of our Lord 180[7].
Sealed and delivered (being first duly stamped) in the presence of [Richard Fauston [sig.] William Paterson [sig.] clerk to Mr Walton, Girdlers' Hall]'.[39]

The duty on apprenticeship premiums between 1710 and 1811 was payable throughout Great Britain under the provisions of an act of Parliament of 1709 (8 Anne, cap. 5), and records of payments of it form the apprenticeship books 1710-1811 amongst the archives of the Inland Revenue in the Public Record Office (PRO class IR 1). These are indexed in a typescript index, known as *The apprentices of Great Britain* 1710-74 (apprentices and masters), compiled for the Society of Genealogists and copies held by the Public Record Office and Guildhall Library. Microfiche copies are also available commercially, and may be held locally.

The apprenticeship books name the apprentice, his parentage (before about 1750 only), the master's name and trade, and dates of the indenture and payment of the duty. They do not include apprenticeships with premiums of less than one shilling (e.g. to family members). *The apprentices of Great Britain* is the only index which approaches a national apprenticeship index, and it is certainly worth checking. Guildhall Library also holds local printed indexes to apprentices, taken from the same records, for Surrey, Sussex, Warwickshire and Wiltshire. Under an act of Parliament of 1694 (5 & 6 Wm. III & Mary II, cap. 10, sect. 6) a stamp duty had already been payable since 24 June 1694 on apprenticeships to livery company freemen in the city of London, and 2s.6d. was collected by the company from each apprentice bound before the company, and passed to the chamberlain of London twice a year, for use in the repayment of the City's debt to the orphans (see chapter 8). Many of the records of these livery company apprentice bindings have been edited by Cliff Webb, as already mentioned (and see appendix 1 for a list of these publications).

As is usual with apprenticeship indentures, each one filed in the city freedom admission papers is one half of what was originally a two-part document. The apprenticeship indenture was printed twice onto a sheet of parchment, head to head. The master signed one, and, in the city of London, the apprentice legally signed the other, even though, at the age of about 14, he was a minor for other purposes. These two copies were cut along the head side, in a zigzag, or curved line, resulting in a toothed, or indented, head edge (hence the term 'indenture'). They acted as carbon copies do today, and could be fitted together again if necessary to check authenticity. The apprentice kept the half signed by the master, and the master kept the half signed by the apprentice in an exchange of contracts. Either half can be present in the city freedom admission papers, and by about the 1830s it is not uncommon to find both halves filed in the relevant monthly bundle of admission papers.

The apprenticeship indenture will always give the apprentice's name, the date he or she commenced the apprenticeship, how long it was to last, and how much of an apprenticeship premium was paid, if any. The apprentice's father (or, very occasionally, mother or other guardian), is named, together with his village or town (sometimes a fuller address) and county of abode, and his occupation. If the father was himself a city freeman, however, he might be described only as 'John Smith, Citizen and [something] of London'. This has the advantage of leading the searcher to look for the father's city freedom admission records, but has the disadvantage of not providing any kind of address for the father.

The apprenticeship indenture will also always note the master's name and city livery company, but hardly ever his actual occupation, or his address. The apprenticeship indentures of some livery companies at some periods routinely give the master's address and real occupation on the printed *pro-forma* apprenticeship indenture forms which they supplied for their apprentices, but instances of this are rare. This information can sometimes be gleaned from documents filed with the apprenticeship indenture in the admission papers. Common additional documents can include a certificate from the livery company stating that the apprentice has been made free of the company on a certain date. Sometimes these certificates give slightly different, or more information: they might give a current address for the apprentice, perhaps, or an address for his master, or trade. By the 19th century, it also becomes common for the master to add a certificate of completion of the apprenticeship, particularly if the master could not attend his apprentice's freedom admission ceremony in person (see plate V for an example).

Sometimes, the original apprenticeship indentures had been lost by both master and apprentice before the apprentice turned up to be admitted to the freedom. In such cases, the admission papers usually contain a certificate from the appropriate city livery company, stating that the apprentice had been bound to his master on a particular date, and that he had subsequently been admitted to the livery company freedom. Such certificates are usually annotated 'L.I.', which is thought to stand for 'lost indenture'.

Other abbreviations which sometimes appear annotated onto the apprenticeship indenture in the admission papers are 'NI' (not inrolled), 'Q' (Quaker), 'BH' (Bridewell Hospital) and 'CH' (Christ's Hospital). Archives of Christ's Hospital (the original 'bluecoat school') are held by the Manuscripts Section of Guildhall Library, and include children's registers 1563-1911 (boys only from 1891), presentation papers 1674-1911 (with gaps; boys only from 1891) and registers of boys and girls discharged and apprenticed 1680-1881. These contain useful genealogical information, depending on the date, such as parentage, parents' marriage, birth and/or baptism of the child and parish of admission. At certain periods only the children of city freemen were admitted to Christ's Hospital, which can lead one back to the city freedom records for a father's city freedom details.

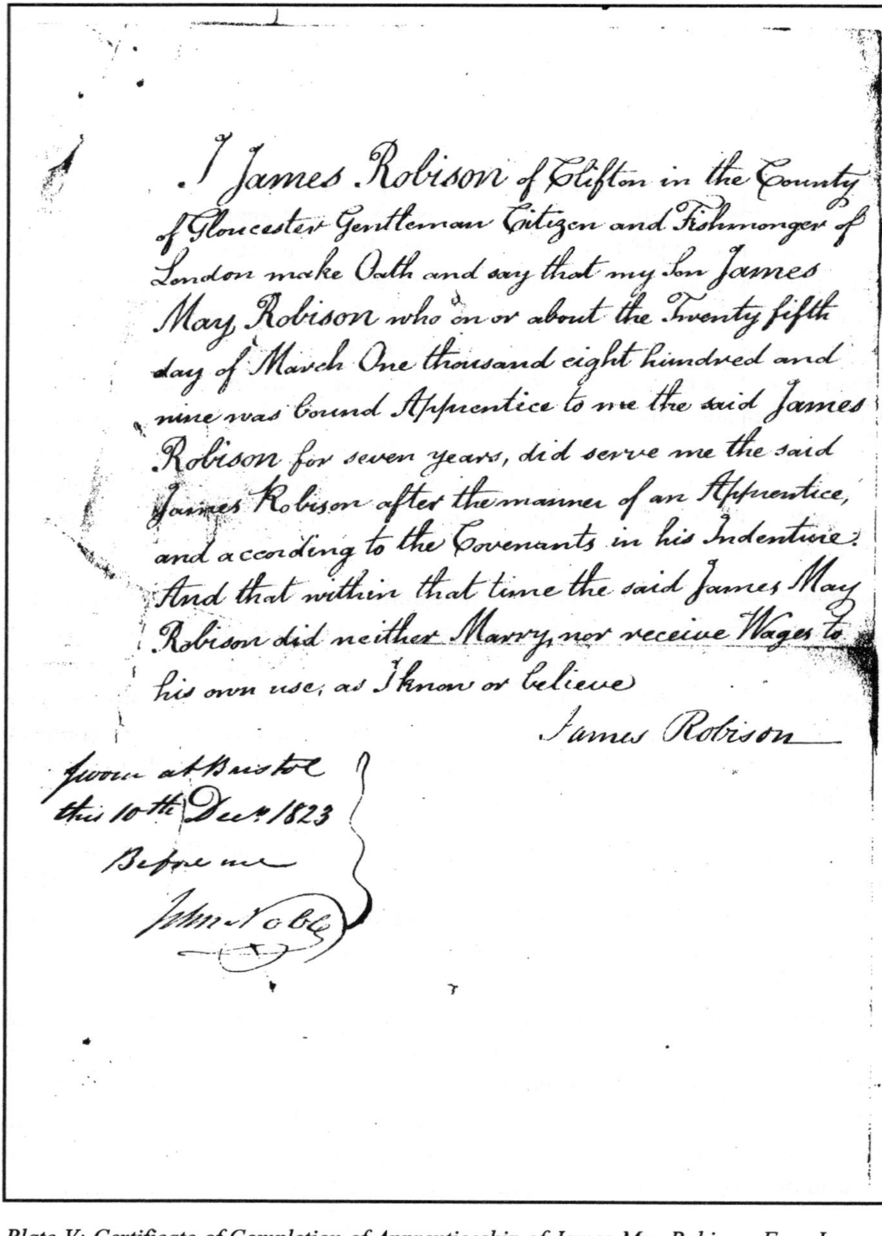

I James Robison of Clifton in the County of Gloucester Gentleman Citizen and Fishmonger of London make Oath and say that my Son James May Robison who on or about the Twenty fifth day of March One thousand eight hundred and nine was bound Apprentice to me the said James Robison for seven years, did serve me the said James Robison after the manner of an Apprentice, and according to the Covenants in his Indenture. And that within that time the said James May Robison did neither Marry nor receive Wages to his own use, as I know or believe

James Robison

Sworn at Bristol this 10th Dec.r 1823 Before me

John Noble

Plate V: Certificate of Completion of Apprenticeship of James May Robison, Free January 1824 [CLRO reference: CF1/1501/18b]

The records of the famous house of correction, Bridewell Hospital, can also be informative. For example, the city freedom admission papers in CLRO for October 1764 contain the apprenticeship indenture of 'Edward Fisher, son of Edward Fisher of the parish of Baksey in the County of Wilts', who with 'the consent of the governors of Bridewell Hospital, London' was apprenticed to Henry Heafford, 'Citizen and Ribbon Weaver of London' to learn the art of a weaver for 7 years from 10 June 1757. On the back of the indenture is a certificate addressed to the chamberlain from the treasurer of Bridewell 'that the within named apprentice Edward Fisher served his apprenticeship to the within named Henry Heafford in Bridewell Hospital and at a court there held the 26th of July [1764] was ordered to be made free of this city'.[40] The Bridewell court of governors' minutes contain references not only to this order to admit him to the city freedom [the governors of Bridewell at this period were appointed by the Corporation of London], but also to Fisher's subsequent petitions for charitable gifts. On 24 April 1765 he petitioned for money from 'Mr Fowkes' gift', stating that he 'had served his apprenticeship in this hospital to Henry Heafford by indenture dated 10 June 1757 and by order of court of 26 July 1764 he was made free of this city the 16 October 1764 and is set up for himself in his said trade [weaver] in Grub Street, the corner of Haberdasher's Square'. His petition was successful, and Fisher, who had 'the character of a diligent and sober man', was allowed £10 on 20 June 1765. Two years later he petitioned for money from 'Mr Locke's gift', by which time he was in trade at 3 Three Cup Alley, Shoreditch, and referred to his former master, Henry Heafford, as 'one of the artsmasters of this hospital'.[41] The artsmasters of Bridewell taught crafts or trades to young apprentices, and this type of training eventually led to the foundation, in 1830, of the House of Occupation 'for the reception of destitute objects of both sexes ... [who were] disposed to work'.[42] Eventually the House of Occupation developed into King Edward's School, Witley, which still exists.

Apprenticeship disputes

Disputes between apprentices and their masters were not uncommon, and the chamberlain of London had jurisdiction over them through the chamberlain's court. Usually this was a question of conciliation between the parties. For example, in 1691, the chamberlain drafted a letter on the back of a scrap of paper which happened later to be used to record the city freedom admission of one John Townsend, in June 1691. The draft letter, however, had nothing to do with Townsend at all: 'Mr Narraway,' wrote the chamberlain, 'There having been a complaint made to me that you do not find the necessary clothes for your apprentice. This is to advise you amicably to end the difference between you, if not, I am willing to give you a hearing at my own house'.[43]

If informal adjudication or a hearing in the chamberlain's court failed to solve the problem, the matter could be taken to the mayor's court, where the apprentice could 'sue out his indentures' and be released from his service to a particular master (see following section). The city chamberlain had the legal right to commit recalcitrant apprentices to a cell in Bridewell for a cooling-off period, and this right was last exercised in 1916, although the jurisdiction has never formally been abolished.

Turnovers to new masters

If there were an insoluble dispute between master and apprentice, or if the master retired, died, or changed occupations, or the apprentice were simply not happy, he could be turned over to a new master. In theory, all such turnovers should have been enrolled by the company and at the chamberlain's court, and details are often found endorsed (written on the back of) the apprenticeship indenture in the city freedom admission papers in CLRO. If there had been a formal dispute which had gone to the mayor's court, then a memorandum of the mayor's court was sometimes either appended to, or endorsed on, the apprenticeship indenture. Whichever means was used, the information usually given is that the apprentice was turned over on a certain date from master A to master B, with the masters' names, companies and sometimes occupation being stated (the new master's occupation is usually merely noted as 'eiusdem arte' [of the same art]). A typical turnover memorandum, in this case separate from the indenture, reads:

> 'Be it remembered that Henry Bateman the apprentice named in the annexed indenture was this day by consent of the parties turned over to Thomas Hacker of Goswell Street, Saint Luke's [parish] in the county of Middlesex timber merchant, a Citizen and Wheelwright of London to learn his said art of a timber merchant for all the now residue of the term of seven years in the said indenture mentioned, there being paid by William Bateman the father of the said apprentice to the said Thomas Hacker as a premium with the said Henry Bateman the sum of four hundred and ninety nine pounds. Dated at Goldsmiths' Hall, London this fifth day of March 1817'.[44]

A typical turnover document from the mayor's court is as follows:

> 'Memorandum that on Wednesday the third day of March 1762 at a court of our sovereign lord King George the third holden before the mayor and aldermen of the city of London in the chamber of the Guildhall of the same city, it was then and there considered and adjudged by the said court that the apprentice in the indenture annexed

named should be wholly discharged from his master therein also named of the remainder of the term of his apprenticeship for that the said master hath left off his trade of a joiner and that he should be turned over to another freeman using the same trade to serve out the remainder of the term of his apprenticeship according to the custom of the said city and the form of a certain petition exhibited by the said apprentice into the said court as by the record thereof fully appears'.[45]

On the back of the attached indenture is written:

54'4th May 1762. Turned over to William Moss Citizen and Carpenter of London to serve the remainder of his term to learn the art of a joiner'.[46]

Records of the mayor's court also exist in CLRO, but are not fully listed for apprenticeship and freedom disputes, and can be hard to use.

If the master died intestate, the record of the turnover will usually contain some reference to 'the consent of the Archbishop of Canterbury': this is due to the fact that the apprentice had to enter into the legal fiction of suing out his indentures by serving the Archbishop of Canterbury (the supposed administrator of the intestate) with a summons, following a petition in the mayor's court. When written out in full, such a document takes on a hint of farce:

'Memorandum that on Friday the second day of December 1763 at a court of our sovereign Lord King George the third holden before the mayor and aldermen of the city of London in the chamber of the Guildhall of the same city. It was then and there considered and adjudged by the said court that the apprentice in the indenture annexed named [George Thomas] should be wholly discharged from Thomas Lord Archbishop of Canterbury to whom the right of administration etc. of John Hunt late Citizen and Cutler of London deceased belongs, of the remainder of the term of his apprenticeship, for that the said archbishop hath left off the trade which the said John Hunt in his lifetime used. And the said apprentice should be turned over to another freeman using the same trade to serve out the remainder of his said apprenticeship according to the custom of the said city and the form of a certain petition exhibited by the said apprentice into the said court ...'.[47]

This is purely a formal administrative procedure: it does not mean that the apprentice or the master is a relation or actual apprentice of the Archbishop of Canterbury.

Pious advice to apprentices

As seen above in chapter 3, each new freeman on admission today receives a copy of *Rules for the conduct of life*, which is based on the type of pious advice to apprentices and servants which became popular in the 18th century. Alderman Sir John Barnard, Lord Mayor 1737-38 is known to have published *A present for an apprentice, or a sure guide to win esteem and an estate, with rules for his conduct to his master, and in the world.* As early as 1660, the chamberlain was giving out to new freemen Richard Younge's books *The heart's index, or self-knowledge* and *A short and sure way to grace and salvation*.[48] Certainly there was a strong tradition in the city, as elsewhere, to give out uplifting literature, especially to apprentices, and there are examples on the backs of pieces of paper subsequently re-used for city freedom admission papers in CLRO, such as the following:

'Instructions for the apprentices in the city of London

'You shall constantly and devoutly every morning and evening in the most humble manner upon your knees worship God, and say your prayers in private by your self: and when you have leisure from your master's business, and shall have your master's leave, you shall go to the public prayers of the church, and there behave your self devoutly and decently. You shall carefully attend to the sermons on the Lord's days, and endeavour to fix them upon your mind, and be sure to practice them in your life and conversation. You shall reverence and obey your superiors and governors. You shall do diligent and faithful service to your master for the time of your apprenticeship, and deal truly in what you shall be trusted. You shall often read over the covenants of your indenture, and see and endeavour your self to perform the same to the uttermost of your power. You shall always avoid evil company, and all occasions that may draw you thereunto; and make speedy return when you shall be sent on your master's or mistress's errands. You shall avoid idleness, and be ever employed, either in God's service, or in your master's business. You shall be of fair, gentle and lowly speech and behaviour to all men; and according to your carriage expect your reward for good or ill from God and your friends. But for your better help and instruction to the performance of your duty, you shall do well, as often to read, and seriously to consider of Holy Scripture, so in particular those passages therein which direct servants how to behave themselves; some few thereof are here inserted, and in special recommended to your frequent perusal and practice, Ephesians the sixth chapter, ver.5,6,7,8, Colossians the third chapter, ver. 22,23,24,25, 1 Epist. to Timothy the sixth chapter, ver. 1,2, Titus the second chapter, ver 9 [hole in document], 1 Epist. of Peter the second chapter, ver. 18, 19, 20, 21. Many more your own diligence may supply. God direct you and assist you in the performance of your duty. God save K William.[49]

7
PATRIMONY

Admission to the city freedom by patrimony gives perhaps the most useful information for genealogists, since details of date of birth and paternity are virtually always given, together with the date of the father's city freedom admission.

To be free of the city by patrimony, a person:

> had to be the legal child of a city freeman (i.e. the child had to have been born in legal wedlock);

> had to be the natural child of a freeman (i.e. not a stepchild or adopted child);

> had to have been born *after* his or her father's (or, after 1976, mother's) own city freedom admission.

Illegitimate children could not claim the city freedom by patrimony, nor could adopted children, even after adoption was first recognised in law by the Adoption of Children Act 1926 (16 & 17 Geo V cap 29).

Before 1976, a person could only claim the city freedom by patrimony through his or her father being a city freeman. Since 1976, a person can claim the city freedom by patrimony through either his or her father or mother, providing that the qualifying parent was free before the child's birth. Since this book is concerned only with records well before 1976, it will refer to the father only as the qualifying parent.

The requirement that a freeman admitted by patrimony had to have been born after his or her father's own admission sometimes causes confusion, although it is really quite straightforward, and even useful for the genealogist. Imagine a married man with one child who then came to London with his family, became a city freeman, and then had other children. The first child, having been born before the father's freedom admission, would not be entitled to claim the city freedom by patrimony, but the subsequent children would be entitled to do so. The principle is the same as that used under Roman law, which gave greater rights of succession to Emperors' children who were 'born in the purple' (i.e. born whilst their father was actually Emperor) than to those born before. The reasoning behind this theory was that, when people were admitted to the city freedom, they became imbued with an 'inchoate right' which they could only transmit to offspring who were born after their admission.

If a person fulfilled all the requirements for admission by patrimony, then no-one could refuse to admit him or her. Like servitude, admission by patrimony was a right, providing that all the criteria were met.

The clerks in the chamberlain's court who made out the papers for city freedom admissions were always careful to record all aspects of qualification by patrimony. Firstly, six guarantors, also known as vouchers or compurgators, had to sign the intending freeman's admission paper (commonly also called the patrimony voucher, rather confusingly) to swear that the person was the legal and natural child of his or her father. This was, in fact, something of a formality, or even a total fiction, for whilst some compurgators were friends or relatives of the intending freeman, the majority were not. It is quite common to find most of the patrimony papers in any given month signed by the same six people, and in these cases it is clear that the compurgators were not necessarily people who had any real link with the intending freeman. Sometimes, the names of the compurgators are those of individuals who are known from other sources to have been staff in the chamberlain's court, or one of the other corporation offices, and so the implication is that they were doing it because they were conveniently close, and probably in order to obtain the small fee payable.

Secondly, the clerks always recorded the father's name, city livery company (if any) and the date on which the father was admitted to the city freedom. This can cut down searches of the alphabets of freedom admissions enormously, as one can go straight to the father's admission papers, knowing that this is the right man, and thus continue back from there. A very lucky searcher might discover several generations of freemen, each made free by patrimony, and thus be able to go back two or three centuries in a fairly short time. This is exceptional, however, and no-one should rely on it happening to them! Sometimes the patrimony paper does not give a full date for the father's freedom admission, but merely a year (requiring a short search of the freedom admission alphabets), with the marginal annotation 'copy'. The clerks often referred to the city freedom certificate as the 'copy of freedom', and so, by extension, this marginal annotation refers to the date of father's freedom.

Not only are the father's details recorded, but the intending freeman's age or date of birth are also routinely given on the patrimony paper after August 1719, when printed *pro-formas* begin to be used for patrimony admissions in the admission papers. These allow space for the place and date of birth to be inserted. However, the clerks did not always write these in the spaces set aside, and it is more common to find the year of birth, sometimes followed by the day and month, underneath the year of father's admission or 'copy'. Sometimes, the freeman's age is written underneath the date of father's copy, and a little sum is done, adding the age of the freeman to the year of father's copy, to make sure it comes to less than the current year, as a kind of double-check that the intending freeman is telling the truth about his or her age, and that he or she was born after the father's admission. At the top of these printed patrimony forms is usually written some indication of where the freeman was born: if the detail is not filled in on the form itself, the letters 'P.O.' or 'P.I.' are scrawled in the top right-hand corner, probably standing for 'patrimony, outside the city' or 'patrimony, inside the city'. A typical post-1719 patrimony paper is illustrated at plate VII. They can easily be recognised in the freedom admission bundles as patrimony papers, as they always carry the Corporation of London's arms at the top of the page.

Before 1719, patrimony admissions are routinely recorded in very abbreviated Latin on small scraps of parchment, which can be hard to decipher. A typical example is given in plate VI, transcribed below:

> *Josephus Webb f[ilius] [Christ]oferi Webb Civis et Pewter[er] Lo[ndini] p[er] Nat[ivitatem] A 10 Oct[obri]s A[nn]o 9 C[aroli] s[ecundi]* ... [list of 7 compurgators' names and livery companies] ... *Bedgrove, C. Bucks. Jurat'*.

and translated thus:

> 'Joseph Webb, son of Christopher Webb Citizen and Pewterer of London [free] by birth [father's city freedom recorded in the book marked with the letter] A [on] 10 October in the 9th year of the reign of [King] Charles the second [i.e. 1657] ... [7 compurgators] ... [freeman born at] Bedgrove, County Bucks. Sworn.'

As with the later patrimony papers, the date of the father's freedom admission is always noted, although the age or date of birth of the freeman is not. The six compurgators also appear, and usually there is a place-name, often near the bottom of the piece of parchment. This is sometimes a city street name, sometimes a village or town outside London, and it is thought that this is probably the freeman's birthplace, rather than address, since the later patrimony *pro-formas* leave space for a birthplace, but never contain a current address.

Additional documents

In common with all means of admission, there are sometimes additional documents to the standard patrimony form in the bundle of admission papers. As with servitude admissions, there is often a certificate of admission to the freedom of the person's city company, if they were being admitted through a company. This can be useful, as

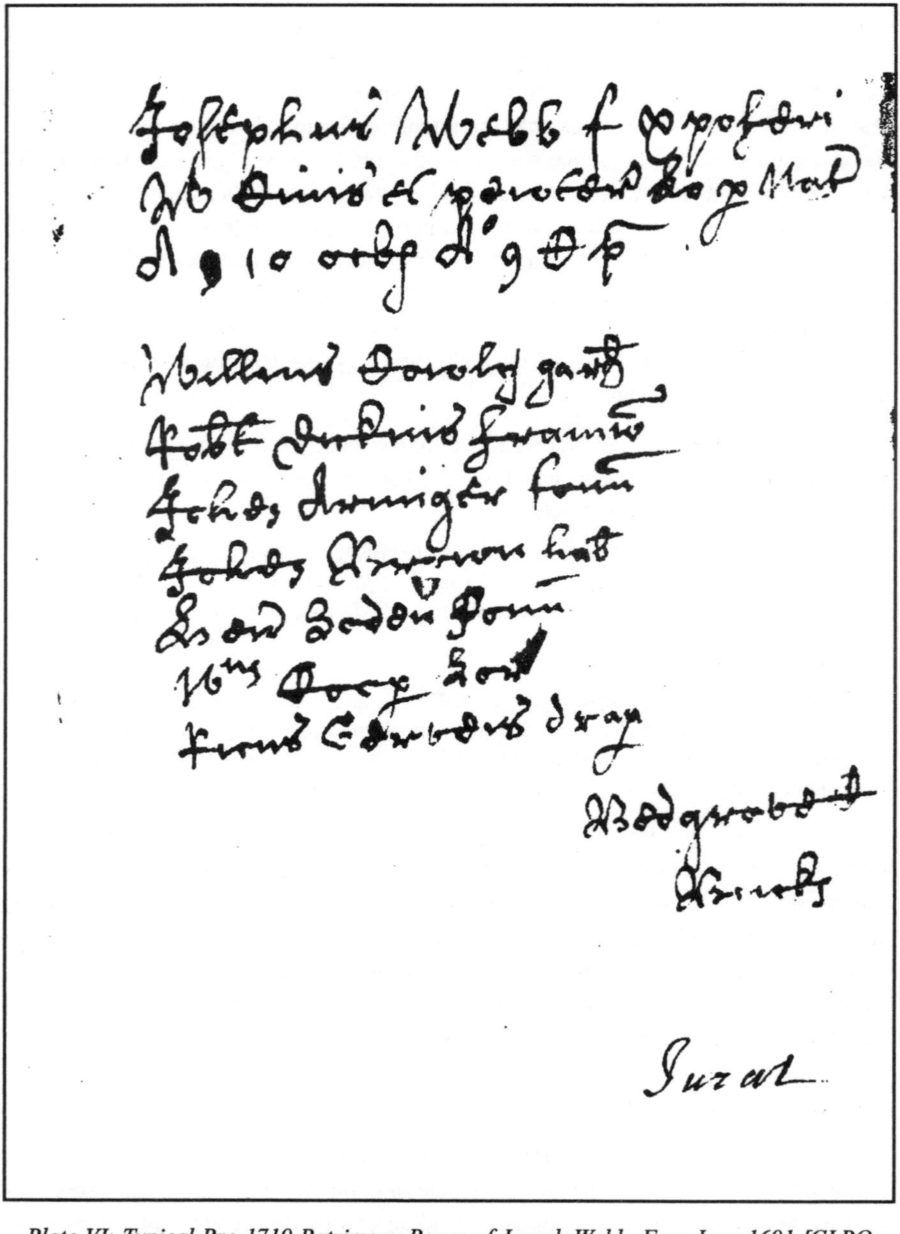
Jurat

Plate VI: Typical Pre-1719 Patrimony Paper of Joseph Webb, Free June 1691 [CLRO reference: ELJL/47/99]

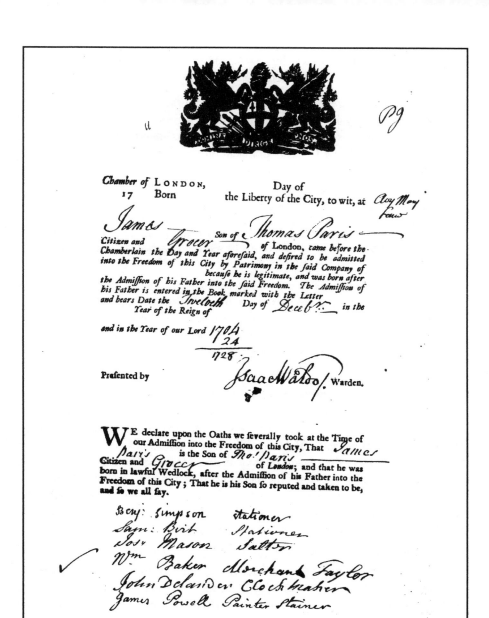

Chamber of LONDON,
17   Born

Day of
the Liberty of the City, to wit, at *Aoy May Low*

James   Son of *Thomas Paris*

Citizen and *Grocer* of London, *came before the*
Chamberlain *the Day and Year aforesaid, and desired to be admitted*
into the Freedom of this City by Patrimony in the said Company of
because he is legitimate, and was born after
the Admission of his Father into the said Freedom. The Admission of
his Father is entered in the Book, marked with the Letter
and bears Date the Twelveth Day of Decb^r: in the
Year of the Reign of

and in the Year of our Lord 1704

24

1728

Presented by   *Isaac Waldo* Warden.

WE declare upon the Oaths we severally took at the Time of
our Admission into the Freedom of this City, That *James*
Paris is the Son of *Tho: Paris*
Citizen and *Grocer* of London; and that he was
born in lawful Wedlock, after the Admission of his Father into the
Freedom of this City ; That he is his Son so reputed and taken to be,
and so we all say.

Benj: Simpson   Stationer
Sam: Birt   Stationer
Jos: Mason   Salter
Wm Baker   Merchant Taylor
John Delander   Clockmaker
James Powell   Painter Stainer

Plate VII: Typical Post-1719 Patrimony Paper, of James Paris, Free August 1746 [CLRO reference: CF1/697/44]

61

the patrimony form does not usually give an address for either the freeman or his or her father, whereas the company certificate might do so.

Sometimes, but very rarely, a certificate of baptism is added to the patrimony form, evidently usually only in the cases where there was some doubt about age, or paternity. An example is that of John Lowder, who was admitted to the city freedom by patrimony through the Cutlers' Company in November 1764. Attached to his patrimony paper is the following oath sworn by his parents:

> 'John Lowder, Citizen and Cutler of London and Ann his wife severally make oath and say that their son John Lowder was born upon the twenty fourth day of February in the year of our Lord one thousand, seven hundred and forty three old stile and that he was privately baptised the same day he was born by the Revd. Mr Bennet, a non-juror clergyman, which was the reason he was not registered in the parish register ... signed John Loader [*sic*] with the mark of Ann Lowder'.

This document has obvious uses to the genealogist. It records not only a date of birth, but also a date and circumstances of a baptism not recorded in a parish register. It also gives the names of both parents, and the signature of the father, and mark of the mother. It has to be emphasised that such documents as this are not very common, even amongst patrimony papers in the city freedom admission papers, but they do sometimes occur.

This particular document dates from after 1752, when the calendar changed so that the new year began on 1 January each year, as it still does today. However, it harks back to the period before 1752, when the year changed on Lady Day [25 March]. Dates between 1 January and 25 March in each year before 1752 can therefore often be ambiguous, unless the person quoting them states whether they are using old style or new style dating, or uses the modern convention of using both old and new style years, separated by a slash. To take the above example, John Lowder the younger was born on 24 February 1743 old style, but 24 February 1744 new style, which we might nowadays write as 24 February 1743/4.

Occasionally, details are recorded of the apprenticeship of a person who was admitted by patrimony. Robert Winder was admitted to the city freedom by patrimony in April 1731. He was aged 21 at the time, and was the son of Robert Winder, Citizen and Merchant Taylor of London, who had himself become a city freeman on 4 August 1703. However, attached to his patrimony paper in the bundle of admission papers is a letter from Robert's master, Balthazar Swartz:

> 'The bearer hereof was bound to me and my late wife to learn her art, which was pattern drawing, my own being painting of faces by ye life, his time being out within

a few months, he has chosen to take up his freedom by his father's copy. I have given my consent to it and delivered him his indentures, would be willing to testify it by appearing at the hall, but am at present so much troubled with the gout that I can't stir out of my chamber, which Mr Mick'l King Citizen and Haberdasher will make oath of if required'.

Also attached to Robert Winder's admission papers is a certificate of his baptism at St Mary Mounthaw on 26 March 1710, he being the son of Robert Winder and his wife Elizabeth.

Oddities

There were some odd aspects of admission by patrimony. One of these was the fact that a person might be able to become free of a livery company by patrimony, but might not be eligible for admission to the city freedom in the same way. George Shaw was a 19th century builder, operating his business from 20 King Edward Street in the city of London. He was also a city common councilman 1868-1896, and should have obtained the city freedom before first standing for election in 1868. However, by accident or design, he did not do so, despite the strict rules about all common councilmen having to be city freemen, although he *did* obtain the quite separate freedom of his livery company, the Plumbers' Company, on 30 June 1851. George had a long and very full civic career: he became a liveryman of the Plumbers' Company, and served as its master several times in the 1880s, although strictly, not being a city freeman, he was not entitled to become a liveryman, let alone master. In his twenty-eight years as a common councilman, he became chairman of the corporation's premier committee, the city lands committee. No-one appeared to notice that he had not been made a city freeman until his son, Henry Ailwyn Shaw, applied for his own freedom of the city by patrimony in 1884. Like many of his generation, Henry had moved out of the city itself, although he still worked there. He was, according to his city freedom application papers, an insurance clerk, working at 7 Royal Exchange, and living at Whit Hern, Cheshunt, Hertfordshire. Henry had been able to obtain his freedom of the Plumbers' Company by patrimony without any problem, because his father had become a freeman of the company in 1851, before Henry was born. But when Henry tried to obtain the city freedom by patrimony, citing the fact that he had been admitted to his livery company freedom by patrimony, a clerk in the chamberlain's court wrote across the top of his application 'Not entitled to the freedom of the city of London by patrimony', because his father had not been admitted to the city freedom at all, let alone before Henry's birth. Poor George, presumably somewhat embarrassed, had to become free of the city himself in September 1884 by redemption, and his son Henry did the same in October 1884, but by redemption, not patrimony.

Although the clerks in the chamberlain's court were usually careful to ensure full compliance with the patrimony rules, a few people occasionally crept into the freedom by patrimony against the rules. One of these was Charles George Nottage, free on 8 January 1885. He had been born at 54 Manchester Street, Islington in 1854, but his father had not been admitted to the city freedom until July 1858. This fact had led to Charles' livery company refusing to allow his admission to the company freedom by patrimony, and so he was admitted to the freedom of the Spectaclemakers' Company by redemption. However, the clerk of the chamberlain's court was probably swayed into admitting him to the city freedom by the fact that Charles' father was the current Lord Mayor, George Swan Nottage A slightly less comprehensible example occurred when Harry Higgs was made free of the Ironmongers' Company by patrimony on 22 April 1909, and of the city, also by patrimony, on 4 May 1909. He had been born at 92 Blythe Street, Bethnal Green, Middlesex on 5 February 1882, but his father, John Alfred Higgs, Citizen and Ironmonger of London, had not been admitted to the city freedom until 8 May 1895.

A person becoming free of the city by patrimony could also do so a very long time indeed after his or her father was admitted. The longest gap between admissions of father and son by patrimony so far found was one hundred and twenty-one years. Robert Albion King, born on 31 October 1824, was admitted to the city freedom on 7 March 1906, at the age of 81. His father, John Henry King, through whom he claimed the freedom by patrimony, had been made a city freeman in 1785.

A child born on the same day as his father's admission was also eligible for admission by patrimony. An example of this was William Phillips Saunders, made free on 9 July 1867. He had been born on 19 November 1844, the same day as the admission of his father, William Henry Saunders.

8

REDEMPTION

Admission by redemption was admission by purchase, and it sometimes seems odd to people today that something they perceive as an honour could be bought with money. However this means of admission is as ancient as any of the others, and indeed it was a vital way of incorporating new blood into the city. There were always many people who either lived in, or came to, London who were not fortunate enough to be children of freemen, or who were not apprenticed to city freemen. Being able to buy into the citizenship enabled such people to become part of the city, and to add their entrepreneurial skills to the city's economy. Unlike servitude or patrimony, however, admission by redemption was always at the discretion of the court of aldermen or (after 1835, in cases where a person was not a company freeman) the court of common council. In most cases of people who became freemen through one of the city companies, it was considered that the company had vetted the person, and so the court of aldermen's permission was usually a formal rubber-stamping procedure. The person obtained the permission of the court of aldermen to be allowed to be admitted, went away and was admitted to the freedom of one of the city companies (if he were not already a freeman of a company), and then came back to the chamberlain's court at Guildhall with his company freedom certificate to be admitted to the city freedom. The typical document in the freedom admission papers in CLRO recording admission by redemption is usually a copy of the order of the court of aldermen (or, after 1835, common council) which allows the person to become a city freeman, and this order was valid for three months (see plate VIII for an example). The date at the top of this order could therefore be up to three months before the date of the person's actual admission date, and this can confuse the unwary researcher, who discovers what they think is the date of freedom admission on a document which they think is in the wrong monthly bundle of admission papers. Like servitude documents, redemption documents virtually never give the exact date of the person's city freedom admission, although they often have accompanying certificates giving the exact date of the city company freedom admission.

The freeman's father's name, address and occupation are usually written sideways down the left-hand margin of the copy orders in the freedom admission papers in CLRO. There is a period about 1800-10, however, when the clerks in the

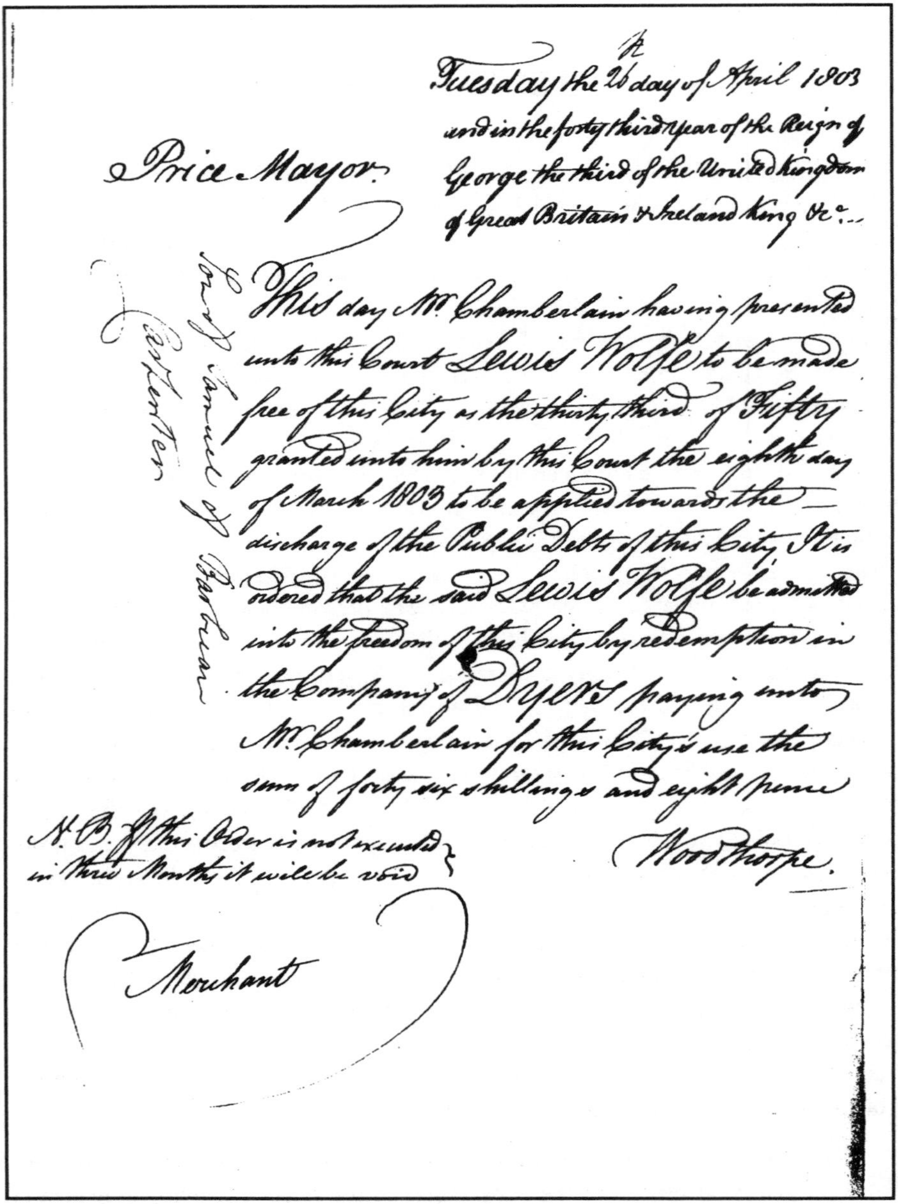

Tuesday the 26 day of April 1803
and in the forty third year of the Reign of
George the third of the United Kingdom
of Great Britain & Ireland King &c...

Price Mayor.

Son of Samuel of Barbican
Carpenter

This day Mr Chamberlain having presented
unto this Court Lewis Wolfe to be made
free of this City as the thirty third of Fifty
granted unto him by this Court the eighth day
of March 1803 to be applied towards the
discharge of the Public Debts of this City It is
ordered that the said Lewis Wolfe be admitted
into the freedom of this City by redemption in
the Company of Dyers paying unto
Mr Chamberlain for this City's use the
sum of forty six shillings and eight pence

Woodthorpe.

N.B. If this Order is not executed
in three Months it will be void

Merchant

Plate VIII: Typical Redemption Order, of Lewis Wolfe, Free April 1803 [CLRO reference: CF1/1272/131a]

chamberlain's court did not include this, for some reason. In these cases, the only means of discovering the father's details is to check the city company archives.

The orders for admission also usually note the freeman's occupation, usually written within a penned circle towards the bottom of the page.

After October 1835, it became possible to become free without the intervention of a city livery company, and a standard application form was introduced for all redemption admissions (see plate IX for an example). This always gives the freeman's name, address and occupation, and between 1835 and 1837, his age as well, although for some reason this was dropped after 1837. It also notes his father's name, address and occupation. In cases where the person becomes free by redemption by being on the parliamentary register (see below), this application form is the only document to be found in the freedom admission papers. For other kinds of redemption admissions, it is additional to the usual orders for admission after 1835, whether through a livery company or not.

Admission by redemption was obtainable in several ways.

Redemption admission by presentation

A person could be presented for admission by a corporation officer or other person who had been granted the right of presenting a limited number of candidates in lieu of salary or as a reward for services. It was assumed that the presenting officer, or other person, would have vetted the intending freeman, to ensure that he or she was a respectable and suitable candidate. The intending freeman might have been a friend or relation of the presenting officer, but it was probably more often the case that the intending freeman had to pay the officer for presenting him or her, in addition to the usual freedom fees, although the city freedom archives do not note this personal fee. For example, when George Steaney, son of William Steaney of Middleton Tyes [Middleton Tyas], Yorkshire, yeoman, was admitted to the city freedom in April 1730, he was presented by the city officer known as the common hunt. The origins of the office of the common hunt (i.e. huntsman) lie in the freeman's ancient right of hunting in Middlesex, and although an officer called the common hunt continued to be attached to the lord mayor's household until 1807, he had long since ceased to be a huntsman by then. On 10 March 1730, the common hunt was granted two freedoms by the court of aldermen, the profits of disposal of which were to be used 'for defraying the expence of providing himself with a new suit of green velvet to be worn on all public occasions for the honour and service of this city'. George Steaney was the freeman who filled the first of these two places, and he presumably paid the

6th day of August 1851

I Ralph Moses Hinds
(Son of Ralph Hinds — late of King street,
Wapping, Carpenter (Publican, &c.?) occupying premises
. 109 Fenchurch Str in the City of London, and carrying on the
. business of a Beer & Bottle Merch do hereby apply
to be admitted to the Freedom of the City of London, by redemption, in pursuance of
the Resolution of the Court of Common Council of the 13th day of July, 1848,
in the Company of Bakers of London ; and I hereby
declare that I am not an Alien, nor the son of an Alien, and that I am above the age of
Twenty-one years.

Witness
Tho. R. Sewell

Ralph Moses Hinds

Plate IX: Typical Post-1835 Redemption Application Form, of Ralph Moses Hinds, Free October 1851
[CLRO reference: CFI/1830/47a]

common hunt half the cost of his new green velvet suit or presenting him, although there is no record of this in the city freedom archives. Such rights of presentation were abolished in the mid 19th century, as corporation officers began to be employed under more modern terms and conditions of service, and no longer purchased their offices, or took perquisites.

In addition to the usual run of presentations as officers' perks, it is common to find a person being admitted 'as the [forty-fourth] of fifty' granted to the chamberlain, and referring to the public debts of the city, for example:

> 'Perring, Mayor
> Tuesday the 20th day of March 1804 ...
> This day Mr Chamberlain having presented unto this court John Whitfield to be made free of this city as the forty-fourth of fifty granted to him by this court on the 26th day of July 1803 to be applied towards the public debts of this city ... '.

The lord mayor for 1803/04 was John Perring, and his name appears at the top left-hand corner of the copy order. The date following ('20 March 1804') is the date of the meeting of the court of aldermen at which John Whitfield was presented for permission to be given for him to be admitted to the freedom. It is not necessarily the same date as his actual city freedom admission. The order was usually valid for three months, within which time the freeman had to go to the chamberlain's court to swear the oath and be admitted by the clerk of the chamberlain's court. 'Mr Chamberlain' is the chamberlain of London. The court of aldermen had granted the chamberlain 50 freedoms on 26 July 1803 (the second date on the document) to present at his discretion. John Whitfield was the forty-fourth person presented by the chamberlain out of that allocation of 50. The date of 26 July 1803 is also nothing to do with the actual date of the freeman's admission, but refers back to the original granting of the 50 freedoms to the Chamberlain.

The public debts of the city is a reference to the city of London's indebtedness to the orphan's fund. The corporation's activities as trustee for the orphans of city freemen are briefly described in chapter 2. However, because of the accounting procedures which were common at the time, the city kept the orphans' money with its own, and did not differentiate when it came to spending money. By 1693, the corporation found itself unable to pay its debt to the orphans, and parliament allowed the corporation to institute an orphans' fund, from its own money and from duties payable on coal and wine, to pay off the debt, under the Orphans' Act of 1694 (5 & 6 Wm. III & Mary II, cap. 10, sect. 6). The stamp duty payable on City apprenticeships after 1694 (see chapter 6) was also paid into the orphans' fund. In addition, as soon as it was realised that the debt would be paid off, other liabilities were made chargeable to the fund, including a number of important improvements. The orphans' debt was finally paid off in 1820, and all outstanding charges upon it were liquidated by 1832, after which it was converted into the London Bridge Approaches Fund, and the coal dues were used for other improvements. The relevance of this to the city freedom admission papers is that the money raised from the chamberlain's 50 freedoms per year went to help pay off the corporation of London's debt to the orphans.

Direct petitions

People without the means or the contacts to become free through presentation could directly petition the court of aldermen (if becoming free through one of the city companies) or the court of common council (if no city company were involved, after 1835, or if the person petitioning were an alien, or the son of an alien, either before or after 1835). This was vital if the person were an alien or the son of an alien (see section on nationality in chapter 3 for details), or if they had broken the terms of their apprenticeship to a city freeman, for example.

Once more, the order of the relevant court allowing their admission is to be found in the freedom admission papers, with the petition. Usually, these petitions are fairly formal affairs, but they can be informative in some cases, particularly where the person to be admitted was an alien or the son of an alien, or where there was a story to tell behind the reasons for admission by redemption (see section on nationality in chapter 3 for examples).

When the person was admitted by petition, bonds were often taken from sureties, or compurgators (up to six of them), who are named on the order for admission, often with the annotation 'taken for security in the mayor's court' plus a date. The requirement for compurgators disappeared in 1856. Like patrimony admissions, it is common in many cases to discover that the same names appear on all the redemption admissions for a particular month, and the inference again is that these sureties were not personal friends or relatives of the freeman, but were acting for a fee, or because they were nearby at the time. In other cases, it is clear that the sureties were indeed relations of the freeman.

Redemption admission by being on the city's parliamentary register of electors

By 1856, the number of new freemen (and the revenue they brought in) was falling, especially since city sworn brokers and licensed victuallers no longer needed to be city freemen from that year. The corporation was also under fairly widespread political attack at this time, and the freedom was being seen by many as an expensive anachronism.

In an effort to make the city freedom more accessible, and to boost the number of freemen, it was ordered in October 1856 that anyone on the city's parliamentary register of electors could henceforth be admitted by redemption. Accordingly, in that same month, some 2,000 people (as opposed to the usual monthly total of 150-200) were admitted to the city freedom, almost all of them by redemption by being on the parliamentary register.

The only document to be found in the freedom admission papers for such parliamentary register (PR) admissions is the standard application form described above in this chapter. The parliamentary register number of the freeman is usually added in the top left-hand corner of the application form and of the freedom certificate. The application form notes the name, address and occupation of the freeman and his father.

9
MAKING A SEARCH

Clearly, this book is aimed at those who had, or probably had, ancestors with some link to the 'square mile' of the city of London. Perhaps those ancestors worked for the Corporation of London, or left a will calling themselves a 'citizen and [something] of London'. For these family historians, searching for ancestors who were freemen of the city of London is a worthwhile exercise, which might yield useful genealogical information.

Before making any search, it helps to have vital dates for the supposed freeman, as the alphabets of admission are arranged in part by date, and a city freeman could only be admitted after the age of 21. Many would have become free at, or soon after, their 21st birthday. On the other hand, some might have waited twenty or thirty years after finishing their apprenticeship to a city freeman. Searches of the city freedom alphabets can be made in person at CLRO, and the appropriate monthly bundles of city freedom admission papers can be seen there, too. Because the alphabets of freedom admissions are arranged partly by date, they can take some time to search, especially if you are searching for a name with a common initial letter: it will always take longer to search through the 'S's than the 'K's for any given period, for example. Give yourself plenty of time, especially if you are searching for more than one person, or if you intend to extract the names of all freemen with a given surname.

Contact the chamberlain's court for information about freemen admitted after 1940, and, if you cannot visit in person, contact CLRO for all freedom admissions before 1940 (see appendix 6 for addresses of these offices). CLRO will answer brief postal enquiries without charge, but only for named individuals with some idea of a date of admission or birth and/or death. CLRO cannot supply details of all persons with a given surname, or where no idea of date is given, as open-ended searches of the alphabets can be very lengthy.

The staff of the chamberlain's court keep all modern freedom admission records on computer, and are in the process of inputting names of former freemen from modern times backwards. However this is a long-term project, and has not yet become useful to people looking for freemen admitted much before 1900. The chamberlain's court do not have facilities for the public to visit to search in person for post-1940 freemen, so you should write to them in the first instance.

The monthly bundles of city freedom admission papers in CLRO were originally thonged through the centre of each document, which can make handling them quite awkward, and copying impossible. However, CLRO, with the help of trained volunteers, is currently undertaking a long-term project to remove the thongs and conserve the documents where necessary, so such handling difficulties should slowly decrease as the project progresses. In the meantime, do not expect copies from thonged or damaged items, and be prepared to handle bundles with great care.

Where there are gaps in the city freedom admission records at CLRO, you can go instead to the records of the supposed freeman's city livery company, if you know it. Do not assume that a person's actual occupation will match their city livery company in every case. Most of the company records are in the Manuscripts Section of Guildhall Library, and appendix 2 lists which records are there, and which are still with the relevant company. If the records are with Guildhall Library, you can search them in person, or write for further information, although again, you will need to keep any written enquiry short and to the point. If the company records are not held by Guildhall Library, you should always write to the company in the first instance, as most do not have facilities for people to visit and research in person, or if they do, an appointment is needed.

Once your freeman ancestor is found, you should be able to obtain from the records some indication of parentage, or place of origin, from either the city freedom, or livery company records. A great many people who became city freemen came from outside London, and this is a splendid source for getting back beyond a family's immigration to London. In some cases, the information given might also lead you to other records, linked to the freedom, such as the city sworn brokers' records or the archives of the City of London Freemen's School in CLRO, or the records of Christ's Hospital in Guildhall Library. Hopefully, this book will have given you some idea of what you might find, and what it might lead to.

APPENDIX 1
USEFUL PUBLICATIONS AND FURTHER READING

Facsimile reprints of maps of London and gazetteers

Most facsimile reprints of maps listed below are available from Guildhall Library Bookshop. Reference copies of the other items are available in CLRO and in Guildhall Library.

16th century:

Prockter, Adrian and Robert Taylor, compilers, with introductory notes by John Fisher, *The A-Z of Elizabethan London* (London Topographical Society Publication No. 122, 1979), indexed.

17th century:

Hyde, Ralph, introductory notes by, and index compiled by John Fisher and Roger Cline, *The A-Z of Restoration London* (Harry Margary, Lympne Castle, Kent, in association with Guildhall Library, London, 1992), indexed.

18th century:

Hyde, Ralph, introductory notes by, *The A-Z of Georgian London* (Harry Margary, Lympne Castle, Kent, in association with Guildhall Library, London, 1981), indexed.

19th century:

Laxton, Paul, introduction by, and index compiled by Joseph Wisdom, *The A-Z of Regency London* (London Topographical Society Publication No. 131, 1985), indexed.

Hyde, Ralph, introductory notes by, *The A-Z of Victorian London* (London Topographical Society Publication No. 136, 1987), indexed.

Map of the city of London Showing Parish Boundaries Prior to the Union of Parishes Act 1907 [based on a late 19th century survey], not indexed [out of print].

Harben, HA *A dictionary of London* (London, 1918).

A list of the streets and places within the administrative county of London (London County Council, various editions at different dates after 1889).

General books about the city and Corporation of London, the city freedom and the city livery companies

Reference copies of all listed below are available in CLRO and Guildhall Library.

The Corporation of London: its origin, constitution, powers and duties (Corporation of London, 1950).

The livery companies of the city of London (Corporation of London, 1997) [Free publication, available from the Public Relations Office, Guildhall, PO Box 270, London EC2P 2EJ].

Aldous, Vivienne E, 'The Archives of the Freedom of the City of London, 1681-1915', *Genealogists' Magazine*, Vol. 23, No. 4 (December 1989) pp 128-133 [this article was written when the CLRO had City Freedom admission papers only up to 1915, but papers up to 1940 have since been deposited in CLRO].

Arnold, Caroline, *Sheep over London Bridge: the freedom of the city of London* (Corporation of London, 1995).

Austin, Evan, *The law relating to apprentices* (London, 1890).

Cooper, CRH, 'The archives of the city of London livery companies and related organisations' in *Archives* XVI, no. 72 (Oct 1984).

Doolittle, IG, *The city of London and its livery companies* (London, 1982).

Hazlitt, W Carew, *The livery companies of the city of London: their origin, character, development and social and political importance* (London, 1892).

Hope, Valerie, *My lord mayor* (London, 1989).

Johnson, David J, *Southwark and the city* (Oxford University Press for the Corporation of London, 1969).

Masters, Betty R, *The chamberlain of the city of London, 1237-1987* (Corporation of London, 1988) [available for sale from the Chamberlain's Court, P.O. Box 270, Guildhall, London EC2P 2EJ, telephone 0171 332 3047 for details of prices and postage charges].

Melling, John Kennedy, *Discovering London's guilds and liveries* (Shire Publications, 1995).

Pulling, Alexander, *A practical treatise on the laws, customs and regulations of the city and port of London* (London, 1842).

Stern, Walter M, *The porters of London* (London, 1960).

Unwin, George, *The gilds and companies of London* (London, 1908).

Calendars and editions of records, biographical dictionaries, and lists of company apprentices, freemen, liverymen, etc.

London's roll of fame 1757-1884 (Corporation of London, 1884).

London's roll of fame 1885-1959 (Corporation of London, 1959).

Who was who, (A and C Black, London, 7 volumes 1935-1981, also available on CD ROM):

1   *1897-1915*
2   *1916-28*
3   *1929-40*
4   *1941-50*
5   *1951-60*
6   *1961-70*
7   *1971-80*

Cumulative index to who was who, 1897-1980 (A and C Black, London, 1981).

A list of the names of the master, wardens, assistants and livery of the Worshipful Company of Clothworkers in London 1788-1803 (no date, held by the Society of Genealogists' library).

'Apprentices and freemen of the Armourers' guild [London] from 1416-1621' in the *Genealogists' Magazine*, vol. 9 (1940-46), pp. 179-192, 217-222.

'Skinners' Company freedoms 1500-1694, including a list of members of the company 1537' in *Miscellanea genealogica et heraldica*, 3rd series, vol. 3 (1900) pp 33-37, 73-76.

Alexander, James MB, *The economic and social structure of the city of London c.1700* A PhD thesis presented to the London School of Economics, University of

London, 1989) [contains a computer print-out index to names and trades in various tax assessments around 1700 (copy held in CLRO for reference purposes only)].

Arber, Edward, ed., *A transcript of the registers of the Company of Stationers of London 1554-1640* (5 volumes, privately printed, 1875-94, facsimile reprint, P Smith, New York, 1950) [includes entries of apprentices and company freemen].

Atkins, Charles Edward, *Register of apprentices of the Worshipful Company of Clockmakers of the city of London from its incorporation in 1631 to its tercentenary in 1931* (privately printed for the company, 1931) [up-dated and complemented by Daniels, see below].

Batchelor, JA, transcriber, typed and indexed by S Doust, *Lists of the court of assistants and liverymen of the Worshipful Company of Cordwainers 1596-1904, transcribed from MSS 2226 and 2191 at the Guildhall Library* (typescript, 1988, held by the Society of Genealogists' library).

Beaven, AB, *The aldermen of the city of London* (London, 2 volumes, 1908, 1913).

Boase, Frederick, *Modern English biography* (1892-1921, reprinted 1965).

Boyd, Percival, *Roll of the Drapers' Company of London: collected from the company's records and other sources* (Croydon, JA Gordon at the Andress Press, 1934).

Boyd, Percival, compiler, *Drapers' Company apprenticeships 1615-1750* (typescript, no date, held by the Society of Genealogists' library).

Boyd, Percival, compiler, *Alphabetical list of the apprentices and freemen of the Company of Stationers of London 1562-1640* (typescript, 1948, held by the Society of Genealogists' Library).

Brown, Joyce, *Notes on mathematical instrument makers in the Grocers' Company 1688-1800 with notes on some earlier makers* (London, Science Museum, 1979)

Christianson, C Paul, *A directory of London Stationers and book artisans 1300-1500* (New York, Bibliographical Society of America, 1990).

Clode, Charles M, *The early history of the Guild of Merchant Taylors of the Fraternity of St John the Baptist, London: with notices of the lives of some of its eminent members, Part 1: The history; Part 2: The lives* (London, 2 volumes, privately printed, 1888) [includes lists of members and wardens of the of the Taylors and Linen Armourers 1392-1700].

Cotterell, H[oward] H[erschel], compiler, *A list of the yeomanry or freemen of the Worshipful Company of Pewterers of the City of London c1687-c1909* (manuscript, 1914, held by the Society of Genealogists' library).

Cotterell, Howard Herschel, *Old pewter: its makers and marks in England, Scotland and Ireland* (Batsford, London, 1929) [includes, on pp 145-344, an alphabetical list of pewterers from the 16th to the early 19th centuries, together with their marks].

Cottrell, Robert J, *The Company of Watermen and Lightermen of the River Thames: apprenticeship binding index 1692-1908, bindings and affidavits 1898-19 49* (9 volumes, on microfiche, available in the Society of Genealogists' library).

Daniels, George, *Freemen of the Worshipful Company of Clockmakers 1631-1984* (Riversdale, Isle of Man, 1984) [updates and complements Atkins, above].

Fothergill, Gerald, transcriber and indexer, typed and an index of masters added by JM Masters, *Apprentices of the Cutlers' Company 1687-1690 and 1712-1719 transcribed from the manuscripts in the Guildhall Library* (typescript, 1973, held by the Society of Genealogists' library).

Fothergill, Gerald, transcriber, typed and indexed by JM Masters, *Apprentices of the Paviours' Company 1565-c1783 transcribed from the manuscripts in the Guildhall Library* (typescript, 1971, held by the Society of Genealogists' library).

[Gandy, Wallace, and JH Bloom, eds.,] *The association oath rolls of the livery companies of the city of London: Apothecaries-Fruiterers,* (unpublished proofs with manuscript corrections and a more modern typescript index [about 1921?]) [held by the Society of Geneaologists, CLRO and Guildhall Library].

Glass, DV, introd., *London inhabitants within the walls 1695* (London Record Society publications, volume 2, 1966). *London inhabitants without the walls 1695* (CLRO, two-volume typescript, not published). 'A supplement to the London inhabitants list of 1695 compiled by staff at Guildhall Library' in *Guildhall studies in London history* volume 2, nos. 2 (part 1, covering surnames beginning A-M) and 3 (part 2, covering surnames beginning N-Z, plus index of trades) (April and October 1976).

Grimwade, Arthur G, *London goldsmiths 1697-1837: their marks and lives from the original registers at Goldsmiths' Hall and other sources* (London, 3rd rev. and enlarged edition, 1990).

Haskett Smith, WP, *The Worshipful Company of Fishmongers: lists of apprentices and freemen in 1537 and 1600-50* (privately printed, 1916).

Heal, Ambrose, *The London goldsmiths 1200-1800: a record of the names and addresses of the craftsmen, their shop-signs and trade-cards* (David and Charles reprint, 1972, of the Cambridge University Press edition of 1935).

Howe, JM, typist and indexer, *Merchant Taylors' Company apprentices, company freemen and masters index 1538-1818* (1988, held by the Society of Genealogists' library).

McKenzie, DF, *Stationers' Company apprentices 1605-40* (Charlottesville, Virginia, Bibliographical Society of the University of Virginia, 1961).

McKenzie, DF, *Stationers' Company apprentices 1641-1700* (Oxford, Oxford Bibliographical Society, 1974).

McKenzie, DF, *Stationers' Company apprentices 1701-1800* (Oxford, Oxford Bibliographical Society, 1978).

Marsh, Bower, *et al*, eds, *Records of the Worshipful Company of Carpenters* (7 volumes, Oxford University Press for the company, 1913-1968), including *Volume 1: Apprentices' entry book 1654-94*, ed. Bower Marsh.

Minet, W and S, eds. *A supplement to Dr WA Shaw's letters of denization and acts of naturalisation for aliens in England and Ireland 1701-1800* (Huguenot Society Publication No. 35, 1932) [includes an index to some previously unindexed pages in *Shaw's Letters of Denization ... 1603-1700,* listed below].

Morgan, Paul, *Warwickshire apprentices in the Stationers' Company of London 1563-1700* (Dugdale Society Occasional Papers No. 25, Stratford upon Avon, 1978).

Page, W, ed. *Letters of denization and acts of naturalisation for aliens in England 1509-1603* (Huguenot Society Publication No. 8, 1893).

Phillips, Henry L, *Annals of the Worshipful Company of Joiners of the city of London* (privately printed, 1915) [includes an alphabetical list of liverymen 1496-1914].

Ridge, C Harold, *Records of the Worshipful Company of Shipwrights: being an alphabetical digest of freemen and apprentices, etc, compiled from Company's records: Volume 1 (1428-1780); Volume 2 (1728-1858)* (Phillimore, London, 1939-1946).

Sharpe, RR, ed., *Calendars of letter books A-L* (1275-1498) (Corporation of London, 11 volumes, 1899-1912).

Shaw, WA, ed. *Letters of denization and acts of naturalisation for aliens in England and Ireland 1603-1700* (Huguenot Society Publication No. 18, 1911) [includes information from some bills which did not pass into acts; partly indexed in W and S *Minet's A supplement to Dr Shaw's letters of denization ... 1701-1800* listed above].

Shaw, WA, ed. *Letters of denization and acts of naturalisation for aliens in England and Ireland 1701-1800* (Huguenot Society Publication No. 27, 1923) [includes information from some bills which did not pass into acts].

Speck, WA and WA Gray, eds., *London pollbooks 1713* in *London politics 1713-1717: minutes of a Whig club 1714-1717 and London pollbooks 1713* edited by H Horwitz and WA Speck and WA Gray respectively (London Record Society Publications, Vol. 17, 1981).

Stephen, Sir Leslie and Sir Sidney Lee, eds., *Dictionary of national biography* (Oxford University Press, 1967-1968, 22 volumes, plus subsequent supplements) also available on CD ROM (Oxford University Press, 1995).

Wall, Col F, compiler, from slips made by G Eland, *Apprentices of the Coachmakers and Coach Harness Makers' of London 1677-1800* (manuscript, held by the Society of Genealogists' library).

Webb, Cliff, *London apprentices* (Society of Genealogists, series from 1996) 15 volumes to date [1998], ongoing:
- *1:*   *Brewers' Company 1685-1800;*
- *2:*   *Tylers and Bricklayers' Company 1612-44, 1668-1800;*
- *3:*   *Bowyers' Company 1680-1806, Fletchers' Company 1739-54, 1767-1808, Longbowstringmakers' Company 1604-1668, 1709, 1714-17;*
- *4:*   *Glovers' Company 1675-79, 1735-48, 1766-1804;*
- *5:*   *Glass-sellers' Company 1664-1812, Woolmen's Company 1665-1828;*
- *6:*   *Broderers' Company 1679-1713, 1763-1800, Combmakers' Company 1744-50, Fanmakers' Company 1775-1805, Frameworkknitters'*

Company 1727-30, Fruiterers' Company 1750-1815, Gardeners'
Company 1764-1850, Horners' Company 1731-1800;

7: Glaziers' Company 1694-1800;

8: Gunmakers' Company 1656-1800;

9: Needlemakers' Company 1664-1801, Pinmakers' Company
    1691-1723;

10: Basketmakers' Company 1639-1824;

11: Distillers' Company 1659-1811;

12: Makers of Playing Cards' Company 1675-1760, Musicians' Company
    1765-1800, Saddlers' Company 1657-1666, 1800, Tobacco
    Pipemakers' Company 1800;

13: Pattenmakers' Company 1673-1805;

14: Spectaclemakers' Company 1666-1800, Loriners' Company 1722-31,
    1759-1800;

15: Gold and Silver Wyredrawers' Company 1693-1837;

16: Tinplate Workers Company 1666, 1668, 1676, 1681, 1683-1800;

17: Innholders' Company 1642-1643, 1654-1670, 1673-1800;

18: Poulters' Company 1691-1729, 1754-1800;

19: Upholdres' Company 1704-1772;

20: Paviors' Company 1568-1800

21: Founders' Company 1643-1800

22: Armourers' and Braziers' Company c.1610-1800

23: Coachmakers' and Coach Harness Makers' Company 1677-1800

24: Ironmongers' Company 1655-1800

Welch, Charles *Register of freemen of the city of London* ..., (London and Middlesex Archaeological Society, 1908), corrected in 'A London manuscript' by Bower Marsh in *The Genealogist,* New Series, XXXII, (Apr 1916) pp. 217-220.

Welch, Charles, *History of the Cutlers' Company of London and of the minor cutlery crafts with biographical notices of early London cutlers, Volume 1: from early times to 1500; Volume 2: from 1500 to modern times* (privately printed for the Cutlers' Company, 1916-1923).

Whitebrook, JC, with W Whitebrook, eds., *London Citizens in 1651: being a transcript of Harleian MS 4778* (London, 1910) [lists liverymen of the city livery companies in about 1651].

Woodhead, JR *The rulers of London 1660-1689: a biographical record of the aldermen and common councilmen of the city of London* (London and Middlesex Archaeological Society, 1965).

Corporation of London schools and other departments

Barty-King, Hugh, *GSMD: a hundred years' performance* (Guildhall School of Music and Drama, 1980).

Carden, Joan, Jean Cardy, Rosemary Hamilton and Anne Savage *Daughters of the city: a history of the City of London School for Girls founded by William Ward* (Corporation of London, 1996).

Douglas-Smith, AE, *The City of London School* (Oxford, 1939, 2nd edition 1965).

Hinde, Thomas, *Carpenter's children: the story of the City of London School* (City of London School, 1995).

Guides

City livery companies and related organisations (Guildhall Library Research Guide 3, 3rd edition, 1989).

City of London parish registers (Guildhall Library Research Guide 4, 6th edition, 1990)

London local archives: a directory of local authority record offices and libraries (Guildhall Library and Greater London Archives Network, 3rd edition, 1994).

London rate assessments and inhabitants lists in Guildhall Library and the Corporation of London Records Office (2nd edition, published by the Library Committee of the Corporation of London, 1968).

Aldous, Vivienne, *City freedom archives* (Corporation of London Records Office Research Guide 1 (2nd edition, 1996) [Free publication available from CLRO].

Aldous, Vivienne, *Sworn brokers' archives* (Corporation of London Records Office Research Guide 2 (1995) [Free publication available from CLRO].

Cox, Jane, and Timothy Padfield, *Tracing Your Ancestors in the Public Record Office* 4th edition, by Amanda Bevan and Andrea Duncan (HMSO, London).

Creaton, Heather, ed., with assistance from Tony Trowles, *Bibliography of printed works on London history to 1939* (London, Library Association Publishing, 1994).

Deadman, H, and Elizabeth Scudder, *An introductory guide to the Corporation of London Records Office* (Corporation of London, 1994).

Gibson, Jeremy, *The hearth tax and other later Stuart tax lists and the association oath rolls* (Federation of Family History Societies in association with Roehampton Institute, London, 2nd edition, 1996).

Gibson, Jeremy, and Heather Creaton, *Lists of Londoners* (2nd edition, Federation of Family History Societies with Centre for Metropolitan History, Institute of Historical Research, London University, 1997).

Gibson, Jeremy, and Colin Rogers, eds., *Poll books c1696-1872: a directory to holdings in Great Britain* (Federation of Family History Societies, 3rd edition, 1994).

Harvey, Richard, *A guide to genealogical sources in Guildhall Library* (Guildhall Library Research Guide 1, 4th edition, 1997).

Jones, Philip E, and Raymond Smith, *A guide to the records in the Corporation of London Records Office and the Guildhall Library muniment room* (English Universities Press, London, 1950).

Lane, RF, *The outwith London guilds of Great Britain* (London, between 1990 and 1994).

Raymond, SA, *Londoners' occupations: a genealogical guide* (Federation of Family History Societies, 2nd edn, 1998).

Raymond, SA, *London and Middlesex: a genealogical bibliography* (Federation of Family History Societies, 2nd edn, 2 vols, 1998).

Webb, Cliff, 'The association oath rolls of 1695' in *Genealogists' Magazine*, Vol. 21, no. 4 (December 1983).

APPENDIX 2
AN ALPHABETICAL LIST OF THE CITY LIVERY COMPANIES

Numbers in round brackets after a company's name indicate its numerical position in the order of precedence. Since the settlement of a violent dispute over precedence in the fifteenth century, the Skinners' and Merchant Taylors' Companies alternate between sixth and seventh place each year.

* indicates that the company's surviving archives, or most of them, are either deposited in the Manuscripts Section of Guildhall Library, or that microfilms are available there. For further details of livery company archives held by Guildhall Library, see *City livery companies and related organisations: a guide to their archives in Guildhall Library* (Guildhall Library Research Guide 3, 3rd edition, 1989). Where companies have retained their own archives, the name and address of the relevant company archivist, clerk or librarian is given at the end of the list.

# indicates that the company was founded after 1940, and therefore people becoming free through such a company will not be found in the pre-1940 freedom admission papers in CLRO. They are listed here only for completeness.

† indicates that the company is no longer in existence, and therefore has no precedent number, but it might be encountered in historical documents such as the city freedom admission papers.

Actuaries (91) #
Air Pilots and Air Navigators (81) #
Apothecaries (58) *
Arbitrators (93) #
Armourers and Brasiers (22) *
Bakers (19) *
Barbers [Barber Surgeons 1540-1745] (17) *
Basketmakers (52) *
Blacksmiths (40) *
Bowyers (38) *
Brewers (14) *
Broderers (48) *
Builders Merchants (88) #

Butchers (24) *
Carmen (77) *
Carpenters (26) *
Chartered Accountants (86) #
Chartered Architects (98) #
Chartered Secretaries and Administrators (87) #
Chartered Surveyors (85) #
Clockmakers (61) *
Clothworkers (12) [archives with company]
Coach and Coach Harness Makers (72) *
Combmakers † *
Constructors (99) #
Cooks (35) *
Coopers (36) *
Cordwainers (27) *
Curriers (29) *
Cutlers (18) *
Distillers (69) *
Drapers (3) [archives with company]
Dyers (13) *
Engineers (94) #
Environmental Cleaners (97) #
Fanmakers (76) *
Farmers (80) #
Farriers (55) *
Feltmakers (63) *
Firefighters (city company awaiting livery) #
Fishmongers (4) *
Fletchers (39) *
Founders (33) *
Framework Knitters (64) *
Fruiterers (45) *
Fuellers (95) #
Furniture Makers (83) #
Gardeners (66) *
Girdlers (23) *
Glass Sellers (71) *

Glaziers (53) *
Glovers (62) *
Gold and Silver Wyre Drawers (74) *
Goldsmiths (5) [archives with company]
Grocers (2) *
Gunmakers (73) *
Haberdashers (8) *
Hackney Carriage Drivers (city company awaiting livery) #
Horners (54) *
Information Technologists (100) #
Innholders (32) *
Insurers (92) #
Ironmongers (10) *
Joiners and Ceilers (41) *
Launderers (89) #
Leathersellers (15) [archives with company]
Lightmongers (96) #
Longbowstringmakers † *
Loriners (57) *
Marketors (90) #
Masons (30) *
Master Mariners (78) [archives with company]
Mercers (1) [archives with company]
Merchant Taylors (alternately 6 or 7) *
Musicians (50) *
Needlemakers (65) *
Painter-Stainers (28) *
Parish Clerks (ancient company without livery) *
Pattenmakers (70) *
Paviors (56) *
Pewterers (16) *
Pinmakers † *
Plaisterers (46) *
Playing Card Makers (75) *
Plumbers (31) *
Poulters (34) *
Saddlers (25) [surviving archives with company]

Salters (9) [archives with company]

Scientific Instrument Makers (84) #

Scriveners (44) *

Shipwrights (59) *

Silkthrowers †* (virtually no archives survive)

Skinners (alternately 6 or 7) *

Solicitors (79) #

Soapmakers †* (virtually no archives survive)

Spectaclemakers (60) *

Stationers (47) [archives with company]

Tallow Chandlers (21) *

Tin Plate Workers (67) *

Tobacco Pipemakers & Tobacco Blenders (82) * (but no membership records survive) [company first founded in 1619, and has had a chequered history since, operating presently under a charter granted in 1960]

Turners (51) *

Tylers and Bricklayers (37) *

Upholders (49) *

Vintners (11) *

Water Conservators (city company awaiting livery) #

Watermen and Lightermen (ancient company without livery) *

Wax Chandlers (20) *

Weavers (42) *

Wheelwrights (68) *

Woolmen (43) *

World Traders (city company awaiting livery) #

Livery company archives not held by Guildhall Library

The archives of the following city livery companies remain in the custody of the company clerks or archivists as follows:

Clothworkers' Company   the Clerk, Clothworkers' Hall, Dunster Court, London EC3R 7AH

Drapers' Company   the Clerk, Drapers' Hall, Throgmorton Street, London EC2N 2DQ

Goldsmiths' Company	the Clerk, Goldsmiths' Hall, Foster Lane, London EC2V 6BN
Leathersellers' Company	the Clerk, Leathersellers' Hall, St Helen's Place, London EC3A 6DQ
Master Mariners' Company	the Clerk, Master Mariners' Hall, HQS 'Wellington', Temple Stairs, Victoria Embankment, London WC2R 2PN
Mercers' Company	the Archivist, Mercers' Hall, Ironmonger Lane, London EC2V 8HE
Saddlers' Company	archives were mostly destroyed by enemy action in 1940. A few items are in the Manuscripts Section of Guildhall Library, whilst the rest are still in the custody of the Clerk, Saddlers' Hall, Gutte Lane, London EC2V 6BR
Salters' Company	the Clerk, Salters' Hall, Fore Street, London EC2Y 5DE
Stationers' Company	the Archivist, Stationers' Hall, Stationers' Hall Court, London EC4M 7DD. There are microfilms of some of the Stationers' Company archives at the St Bride Printing Library, Bride Lane, London EC4Y 8EE, but an appointment is necessary for access to these.

APPENDIX 3
SOME USEFUL GENEALOGICAL SOURCES IN THE CORPORATION OF LONDON RECORDS OFFICE

City freedom archives most useful to the genealogist

City freedom admission papers 1681-1940 (over 2,800 bundles), indexed by volumes of alphabets (13 volumes).

City freedom books (*alias* registers or declaration books or the 'chamberlain's books') 1784-1997 (145 volumes) (freedom books 1930-41 destroyed by enemy action), effectively indexed as to month of admission by the alphabets to the admission papers (13 volumes).

Apprenticeship inrolment [*sic*] books 1786-1974 (16 volumes, 1913-1940 on microfilm only) (inrolment book 1914-40 destroyed by enemy action, but a contemporary microfilm of it is held by CLRO), indexed by volumes of alphabets 1786-1959 (9 volumes).

Wardmote inquest returns of non-freemen 1821-53 (8 volumes, the earliest of which (1821-28) is too fragile to handle), indexed.

Apprenticeship complaint books 1786-1917 (18 volumes), each volume indexed 1801-1917.

'King's freemen's' discharge papers, late 18th-early 19th century, about 4,000 items, indexed.

City Imperial Volunteer Archives in the Corporation of London Records Office

Reports on the raising, organising, equipping and despatching the City of London Imperial Volunteers to South Africa, published by order of the Rt. Hon. the Lord Mayor, Sir Alfred J. Newton, Bart. (London, June 1900) [CLRO reference: CIV/1/10].

Also various CIV albums, scrapbooks and diaries of a few individual CIVs, together with photographs, press cuttings, cap badges, insignia, medals and other memorabilia; menus for reunion dinners 1900-1964; reports and published material.

Licensed non-free journeymen

Licence books 1750-1845 (10 volumes, indexed for both masters and journeymen 1750-61 and for masters only 1761-1810).

Records of corporation schools

City of London school pupils 1837-1900 (3 volumes, plus index volume).

City of London Freemen's School Register 1853-1955 (1 volume, 75 year closure period).

City of London Freemen's School application forms 1853-1943 (75 year closure period).

Guildhall School of Music and Drama student record cards for pupils back to about the period of the First World War (1914-18), probably not complete (card index and alphabetically arranged binders, 75 year closure period).

Orphans' inventories

Orphans' inventories 1662-1742, 1764-1773 (indexed).

City of London sworn brokers 1285-1886

[CLRO publishes a free research guide on the sworn brokers, available on receipt of an A5 stamped self-addressed envelope].

1285-1498: Letter books (edited and printed as *Calendars of Letter Books A-L (1275-1498)*, edited by RR Sharpe (London, 11 volumes, 1899-1912, indexed)).

1495-1697: Repertories of the court of aldermen (subject indexed).

Index to brokers' bonds (1697-1870, with a few from 1650).

Registers of brokers admitted (1708-1869).

Registers of brokers admitted, discharged and deceased (1772-1886).

Printed lists of brokers' names and addresses 1804-82, with many gaps. [Guildhall Library also has such lists 1797-1886 (with many gaps)].

Ledgers of brokers' rents (1708-1886).

Notices of discharge (indexed, 1863-73 only).

Jewish and alien brokers: petitions for admission (c.1708).

Register of Custom House agents recommended by the lord mayor 1823-56.

Brokers' medals (1803, 1837-61), Receipts for brokers' medals (1840-62, not indexed). Some city licensed brokers' medals are illustrated and discussed in 'Brokers' Medals and Stockbrokers' Tokens', by JB Caldecott, in the *Stock Exchange Christmas Annual*, (1905-06), pp. 231-241. CLRO and Guildhall Library have a copy of this article.

City of London sessions, transportation and emigration records

[CLRO publishes a free research guide on these records, available on receipt of an A5 stamped self-addressed envelope. It includes details of published indexes to the records listed below.]

London sessions minute books 1612-1834 (large gaps before 1666, indexed 1714-1834).

London sessions files 1610-1834.

London sessions papers (gaol delivery and peace) 1648-1785.

London sessions papers (peace only) 1787-1971.

Old Bailey sessions papers (OBSP) 1777-1834 (with gaps) [a fuller series, 1684-1913 (with gaps) is held by the Printed Books Section of Guildhall Library].

Southwark sessions papers transportation bonds 1746-73.

Southwark compter commitments 1814-42 (indexed 1815-42)

Southwark quarter sessions of the peace minute books 1666/7-1929 (rough minutes only after 1791).

Southwark sessions files 1667-1870.

Southwark sessions papers 1654-1784 (with gaps).

Lists of convicts on board ships to Australia 1829-40 from the United Kingdom and the British West Indies (not indexed).

Inhabitants' lists

[CLRO publishes a free information leaflet on these records, available on receipt of a stamped self-addressed envelope.]

Tax assessments (including poll, hearth, land, window, tithe, marriage, birth and burial taxes, mostly for the city of London) late 17th-early 19th centuries (mostly 1673-98). [Guildhall Library Manuscripts Section also holds a number of tax assessments for the city of London.]

Poll and scrutiny books for the City of London for the following elections and dates (poll books unless otherwise stated):

parliamentary elections 1792 (livery list, checked against poll books of previous contested election), 1796;

aldermanic elections (Langbourn Ward) 1712 (scrutiny and return books), 1823;

common council elections [1719/20?], 1722/23 (both for Cripplegate Ward Without, both scrutiny books), 1717 (Tower Ward);

election of lord mayor 1772;

election of bridgemaster 1771.

Other city of London poll books held elsewhere are listed in J Gibson and C Rogers *Poll Books c1696-1872* (see appendix 1 for details).

Rate books 1908-85 (appointment advisable at least 24 hours in advance, access controlled) [pre-1908 rate books for the city, and for individual wards and parishes, are held by Guildhall Library].

Rates valuation lists 1862-1956 (with gaps) [no access problems].

City of London parliamentary electoral registers 1840, 1872 to date (gaps 1897-98, 1903-04, 1916-17,1940-44) [Guildhall Library also holds copies 1832 to date (gaps 1916-17, 1941-44)].

Ward registers 1946/47-1948/49 (a few wards only), 1950 to date [copies also held by Guildhall Library 1950 to date].

Common hall registers 1887/88 to date (1940/41 missing) [copies also held by Guildhall Library].

Coroners' inquests for the city of London and ancient borough of Southwark

[CLRO publishes a free information leaflet on these records, available on receipt of a stamped self-addressed envelope; request this for details of London and Southwark coroners' inquests before 1788. See also Gibson, J, and C Rogers, *Coroners' Records in England and Wales*, (Federation of Family History Societies, 2nd edition, 1997)].

London coroners' inquests and depositions 1788-1992 (75 year closure period; all available inquests indexed; includes Holloway prison inquests 1852-1965).

Borough of Southwark coroners' inquests and depositions 1788-1932 (75 year closure period; all available inquests are indexed).

Prison inquests (including Newgate, Bridewell, Ludgate, the Fleet and the Compters) 1783-1839 (with gaps).

Corporation of London members and employees

Corporation annual pocket books 1788 to date (with gaps, especially in the earlier period).

Returns of officers, mainly 18th-20th centuries.

Indexes to lord mayors, sheriffs, aldermen and common councilmen 12th century to date.

Miscellaneous biographical notes.

Market tenants, porters and drovers

Billingsgate Market porters' licences 1877-1906, 1908-48 (indexed).

Billingsgate and Leadenhall Markets rental of tenants 1876-1907 (not indexed)

Metropolitan Meat and Poultry Market tenants 1872-87, applications for space 1868-76 and rental of tenants of about 1864-75.

London Central Markets tenants 1875-1955.

London Central Markets porters' licences 1904-27.

Metropolitan Cattle Market tenancy agreements 1872-87.

Metropolitan Cattle Market drovers' licences 1854-1963 (indexed 1854-1936).

Spitalfields Market tenants 1906-20.

APPENDIX 4
LIST OF INDIVIDUALLY GRANTED HONORARY FREEDOMS

The list of individual honorary freemen below is taken mostly from *London's Roll of Fame 1757-1884* and *London's Roll of Fame 1885-1959* (Corporation of London 1884 and 1959 respectively), and from the list in the chamberlain's court of the Corporation of London, checked against the common council minutes after 1959. The earliest freemen on this list are not included in *London's Roll of Fame 1757-1884*, and the information on them has been taken from Betty Masters *The chamberlain of the city of London, 1237-1987* (Corporation of London, 1988), and records in CLRO. Any other information not included in these sources has come from other records in CLRO.

Note that not everyone who was voted the freedom was necessarily admitted. In particular, officers of the Royal Navy during the Napoleonic Wars, or soldiers serving in India and elsewhere in the 19th century were often voted the honorary freedom, but could be away for years at a time, or might have died before they had an opportunity to attend Guildhall and be admitted. The list is annotated accordingly in such cases, although in some cases, it is not known for certain whether a person was admitted or not. The freedom books in CLRO only survive after 1784, and for most honorary freedoms, there are routinely no papers in the monthly bundles of admission papers either. If there is also no newspaper, or other account of the proceedings, then there can be no record of admission at all.

Military and naval recipients were usually given a sword to accompany the grant of the honorary freedom. Other recipients often received their certificate of admission in a box made of gold or heart of oak.

Alien recipients, who were not subjects of Britain or the Empire (or subsequently the Commonwealth), could not take the freeman's oath or declaration of allegiance to the British monarch, and were therefore technically not admitted to the city freedom. However, they are included on this list, appropriately annotated, as they were voted the honour, and are generally regarded as honorary freemen.

The corporation also often voted addresses of welcome to visiting heads of state, or to reigning monarchs, to whom (after King Charles II) it was not considered appropriate to offer the honorary city freedom. These are not included in this appendix, but for 1757-1959 they can be found at the back of the two volumes of *London's roll of fame*.

Date of admission to the honorary city freedom	Recipient of honary city freedom
29 Oct 1674	HM King Charles II
	HRH James, Duke of York (afterwards King James II)
17 Dec 1736	HRH Frederick Louis, Prince of Wales
[?] Aug 1746	HRH William Augustus, Duke of Cumberland [voted the honorary freedom on 23 January 1745/6, but no evidence found of exact date of admission: see plate III for common council order to admit him]
24 May 1757	Rt. Hon. William Pitt MP (afterwards Earl of Chatham)
	Rt. Hon. Henry Bilson Legge MP
18 Feb 1761	George Cooke MP
7 May 1761	Sir John Philipps MP
11 June 1761	Rt. Hon. Arthur Onslow, Speaker of the House of Commons
31 July 1761	HRH Edward Augustus, Duke of York and Albany, Rear-Admiral of the Blue Squadron of HM's Fleet
7 March 1764	Rt. Hon. Sir Charles Pratt, Chief Justice of the Common Pleas (afterwards Earl Camden)
6 June 1765	HRH The Duke of Gloucester
18 Dec 1765	HSH The Hereditary Prince of Brunswick Lunenburg
12 Mar 1767	HRH Henry Frederick, Duke of Cumberland
	Rt. Hon. Charles Townshend MP [voted the honorary freedom on 23 June 1767, but died before he could be admitted]
	HM Christian VII, King of Denmark [voted the honorary freedom on 10 October 1768, but as an independent sovereign he could not take the oath of allegiance to the British crown, and thus he was technically not admitted to the city freedom. His resolution and gold box were delivered to the Danish Ambassador]

12 Mar 1767 John Dunning, ex-Solicitor-General (afterwards Baron Ashburton)
[voted the honorary freedom on 12 October 1770 for defending in Parliament 'the right of the subject to petition and remonstrate', but no evidence found of admission]

Rev. Richard Price DD, FRS
[voted the honorary freedom on 14 March 1776 for his book *Observations on the nature of civil liberty, etc*, but no evidence found of admission]

26 Mar 1777 David Hartley
[statesman and inventor, awarded the honorary city freedom 'for his inventions for securing buildings from fire']

Rt. Hon. Sir Fletcher Norton, Speaker of the House of Commons (afterwards Baron Grantley).
[voted the honorary freedom on 14 May 1777, but no evidence found of admission]

11 Dec 1779 Hon. Augustus Keppel, Admiral of the Blue

Rear-Admiral Sir George Brydges Rodney (afterwards Lord Rodney)
[voted the honorary freedom on 6 March 1780, but no evidence found of admission]

Sir Henry Gould, one of the judges of the Court of Common Pleas
[voted the honorary freedom on 19 June 1780 for his opposition to the establishment of martial law during the Gordon Riots of 1780, but no evidence found of admission]

Rt. Hon. Lord Hood, Rear-Admiral of the Blue.
[voted the honorary freedom on 20 [not 22] June 1782, but no evidence found of admission]

Rear-Admiral Sir Francis Samuel Drake
[voted the honorary freedom on 20 [not 22] June 1782, but no evidence found of admission]28 Feb 1784

Rt. Hon. William Pitt MP

5 Apr 1794 Marquis Cornwallis, Commander-in-Chief of HM's Forces in the East Indies

17 May 1794 Major-General Sir William Meadows KCB

Major-General Sir Charles Grey KCB (afterwards Viscount Howick and Earl Grey)
[voted the honorary freedom on 27 May 1794, but no evidence found of admission]

Vice-Admiral Sir John Jervis KCB (afterwards Earl St Vincent)
[voted the honorary freedom on 27 May 1794, but no evidence found of admission]

6 May 1796	Rt. Hon. Earl Howe, Admiral of the White, Vice-Admiral of England and Commander of HM's Fleet in the Channel
	Vice-Admiral Sir Charles Thompson. [voted the honorary freedom on 10 Mar 1797, but died before he could be admitted: resolution and box presented to his widow]
6 May 1796	Rear-Admiral Parker [voted the honorary freedom on 10 March 1797, but no evidence found of admission]
28 Nov 1797	Commodore Horatio Nelson (admitted as Rear-Admiral Sir Horatio Nelson, afterwards Lord Viscount Nelson, Vice-Admiral of the Blue)
5 Dec 1797	Vice-Admiral the Hon. William Waldegrave
6 Feb 1798	Rt. Hon. Alexander Hood, Lord Bridport, Vice-Admiral of England
22 May 1798	Admiral Lord Viscount Duncan
11 Dec 1798	Vice-Admiral Sir Richard Onslow
2 May 1799	Captain Sir Robert Calder RN
27 May 1799	Sir John Borlase Warren KCB [awarded the honorary city freedom for his victory in 1798 against the French fleet transporting troops to support the rising in Ireland]
8 Aug 1799	Captain Edward Berry RN
6 Feb 1800	Vice-Admiral Andrew Mitchell
2 May 1800	Lieutenant-General Sir Ralph Abercromby KCB
29 May 1800	Captain Sir Edward Hamilton RN
	William Adams [voted the honorary freedom on 4 November 1800 for supplying cheap potatoes from his premises in Honey Lane Market for the relief of the poor, but no evidence found of admission]
	Lieutenant-General the Hon. Sir John Hely Hutchinson KCB [voted the honorary freedom on 19 November 1801, but no evidence found of admission]
17 Dec 1801	Captain Sir William Sidney Smith RN
1 Oct 1802	Admiral Lord Keith
8 Mar 1803	Rear-Admiral Sir James Saumarez, KCB (afterwards Baron De Saumarez)
4 Jul 1805	Dr Edward Jenner [awarded the honorary city freedom for his work on innoculation against smallpox]

Vice-Admiral Lord Collingwood
[voted the honorary freedom on 26 Nov 1805, but died before he could be admitted: sword presented to his widow]

Captain Thomas Masterman Hardy RN (afterwards created a baronet)
[voted the honorary freedom on 30 January 1806, but no evidence found of admission]

Rear-Admiral Sir Thomas Louis
[voted the honorary freedom on 27 Mar 1806, but died before he could be admitted: resolution and sword presented to his son, Captain Sir John Louis]

Lieutenant-General Sir David Baird KCB
[voted the honorary freedom on 2 October 1806, but no evidence found of date of admission]

8 Jan 1808 Commodore Sir Home Popham

Major-General Sir John Stuart KCB

18 Apr 1808 Brigadier-General Sir Samuel Auchmuty

17 June 1808 Vice-Admiral Sir John Thomas Duckworth GCB

Gwyllim Lloyd Wardle MP
[voted the honorary freedom on 6 April 1809 for his Parliamentary attacks culminating in the retirement of Frederick, Duke of York as Commander-in-Chief, on the grounds that he had been granting commissions through his mistress, but no evidence found of admission]

23 Apr 1810 Brigadier-General The Hon. William Lumley

Rear-Admiral Charles Stirling

7 June 1810 William Rogers
[late Acting Captain of the *Windsor Castle* packet, awarded the honorary city freedom for his defence of his vessel, and his capture of the attacking French privateer *Le Genii* on 1 October 1807]

16 July 1810 Rear-Admiral The Earl of Northesk

Rear-Admiral Sir Richard John Strachan

HRH The Prince Regent (afterwards King George IV)
[voted the honorary freedom on 2 May 1811, but he refused admission]

12 Dec 1811 Brigadier-General William Thomas Dilkes

13 Dec 1813 Rear-Admiral the Hon. Alexander Cochrane

19 May 1814 Captain PBV Broke RN

11 June 1814 Lieutenant-General Sir Rowland Hill (afterwards Lord Viscount Hill)

11 June 1814	Major-General Sir William Carr Beresford (afterwards Lord Viscount Beresford)
9 July 1814	Lieutenant-General Lord Viscount Wellington (afterwards Field Marshal The Duke of Wellington)
27 Mar 1815	Lieutenant-General Sir Thomas Graham
11 July 1816	HRH The Duke of Kent
	HRH The Duke of Sussex 11 July 1816 HRH The Duke of Gloucester
	HSH Leopold George Frederick, Duke of Saxe-Coburg (afterwards King of the Belgians)
31 Jan 1817	Admiral Lord Viscount Exmouth GCB
	Rear-Admiral Sir David Milne KCB
23 Mar 1820	The Most Noble The Marquis Camden
2 June 1821	Henry Brougham MP (afterwards Baron Brougham and Vaux and Lord Chancellor), Queen Caroline's Attorney-General [awarded the honorary city freedom for his efforts in defence of Queen Caroline against her divorce from King George IV]
	Thomas Denman MP (afterwards Lord Denman and Chief Justice of England), Queen Caroline's Solicitor-General [awarded the honorary city freedom for his efforts in defence of Queen Caroline against her divorce from King George IV]
	Stephen Lushington MP, DCL (afterwards Sir Stephen Lushington, Judge of the Admiralty Court) [awarded the honorary city freedom for his efforts in defence of Queen Caroline against her divorce from King George IV]
21 Feb 1822	Joseph Hume MP
8 Apr 1829	Rt. Hon. Robert Peel MP (afterwards Sir Robert Peel)
9 July 1831	Rt. Hon. Lord John Russell MP (afterwards Earl Russell KG)
23 May 1832	Thomas Attwood [awarded the honorary city freedom for services in the cause of Parliamentary reform, and his 'uniting [of] the intelligent and industrious artizans, and the inhabitants generally of the midland districts, in their firm but peaceable pursuit of that great national object']
11 July 1832	Rt. Hon. Earl Grey
11 July 1832	Rt. Hon. Viscount Althorp MP (afterwards Earl Spencer)
27 Mar 1834	Captain John Ross RN (afterwards Rear-Admiral Sir John Ross KCB)

Andrew Stephenson, American Minister in London
[voted the honorary freedom on 16 February 1838, but he refused admission on the grounds that it was incompatible with his public office]

15 Apr 1839   Thomas Clarkson MA
[philanthropist, awarded the honorary city freedom for his services in the cause of the abolition of slavery]

7 Apr 1840   Sir Thomas Phillips, Mayor of Newport, Monmouthshire
[repelled a Chartist attack on Newport]

21 May 1840   Lieutenant-General Sir John Colborne GCB (afterwards Lord Seaton)

28 Aug 1840   HRH Prince Albert KG, Prince Consort

23 Sep 1841   Admiral The Hon. Sir Robert Stopford GCB

Commodore Sir Charles Napier KCB (afterwards Vice-Admiral)

25 Nov 1841   Major-General Sir Charles Felix Smith

17 Mar 1842   HRH The Duke of Cambridge

Major-General Sir Robert Henry Sale GCB
[voted the honorary freedom on 12 Dec 1844, but died before he could be admitted]

Major-General Sir William Nott GCB
[voted the honorary freedom on 12 Dec 1844, but died before he could be admitted: resolution and silver cup sent to his widow]

17 July 1845   Major-General Sir Henry Pottinger GCB

20 May 1847   Major-General Sir Henry George Wakelyn Smith KCB

29 Oct 1847   His Excellency James Brooke, Rajah of Sarawak (afterwards Sir James Brooke KCB)

17 Dec 1847   Major-General Sir George Pollock GCB

13 Apr 1848   Lieutenant-General The Rt. Hon. Sir Henry Hardinge GCB (afterwards Lord Viscount Hardinge, Field Marshal and Commander-in-Chief)

20 July 1848   Robert Pitt Edkins MA, Second Master of the City of London School

31 Oct 1848   Rev. George Ferris Whidborne Mortimer DD, Headmaster of the City of London School

30 May 1850   General Sir Hugh Gough GCB (afterwards Lord Viscount Gough)

9 Feb 1854   Austen Henry Layard DCL, MP
[awarded the honorary city freedom for his services to archaeology]

Sir Jamsetjee Jeejeebhoy
[voted the honorary freedom on 14 April 1855, but as he could not attend

Guildhall to be admitted, the illuminated resolution was sent to him in Bombay]

19 May 1856   Admiral Sir Edmund Lyons GCB (afterwards Lord Lyons)

31 July 1856   Major-General Sir William Fenwick Williams GCB

21 May 1857   Rev. David Livingstone LL.D

13 July 1857   HRH Prince Frederick William of Prussia (afterwards Crown Prince of Germany)
[voted the honorary freedom on 27 June 1857, but as an alien he could not take the oath of allegiance to the British crown, and thus he was technically not admitted to the city freedom. He attended Guildhall and was presented with a copy of the resolution in a gold box on 13 July 1857]

4 Nov 1857   HRH The Duke of Cambridge, Commander-in-Chief

3 June 1859   Sir John Laird Mair Lawrence GCB (afterwards Baron Lawrence of the Punjab)1 Mar 1860Rt. Hon. The Earl of Elgin and Kincardine KT

19 May 1860   Captain Sir Francis Leopold McClintock RN (afterwards Vice-Admiral)

20 Dec 1860   Rt. Hon. Colin, Baron Clyde GCB, DCL

20 Dec 1860   Lieutenant-General Sir James Outram GCB

6 June 1861   Richard Cobden MP

Rt. Hon. the Earl Canning
[voted the honorary freedom on 5 June 1862, but died before he could be admitted: resolution presented to his sister]

10 July 1862   George Peabody
[voted the honorary freedom on 22 May, and attended Guildhall on 10 July 1862, but as an alien (an American) he could not take the oath of allegiance to the British crown, and thus was technically not admitted to the city freedom]

8 June 1863   HRH Albert Edward, Prince of Wales KG, etc.

20 Apr 1864   General Giuseppe Garibaldi
[voted the honorary freedom on 7 April, and attended Guildhall on 20 April 1864, but as an alien he could not take the oath of allegiance to the British crown, and thus he was technically not admitted to the city freedom]

7 June 1866   HRH Prince Alfred, Duke of Edinburgh KG, etc.

21 July 1868   Major-General Sir Robert Napier (admitted as the Rt. Hon. Baron Napier of Magdala and Caryngton GCB, GCSI)

22 Oct 1868   Field Marshal Sir John Fox Burgoyne GCB

30 July 1870   M. Ferdinand de Lesseps (Viscount of France)
[voted the honorary freedom on 11 July 1870, and attended Guildhall on

30 July 1870, but as an alien he could not take the oath of allegiance to the British crown, and thus he was technically not admitted to the city freedom]

13 July 1871   HRH Prince Arthur (afterwards Duke of Connaught KG)

18 July 1872   Rt. Hon. Angela Georgina, Baroness Burdett-Coutts
[philanthropist, awarded the honorary city freedom for her gift to the Corporation of London of Columbia Market]

6 Nov 1873   Sir Albert David Sassoon KCSI
[awarded the honorary city freedom for his services to education, especially in India]

16 July 1874   Sir Henry Bartle Edward Frere GCSI, KCB
[awarded the honorary city freedom for his public services in India, and for his work towards the treaty with the Sultan of Zanzibar for the abolition of slavery on the east coast of Africa]

22 Oct 1874   Major-General Sir Garnet Joseph Wolseley KCB, GCMG (afterwards Baron Wolseley of Cairo)
[also presented with an address of thanks and congratulation in a gold box on 11 April 1883 for services in Egypt]

25 Oct 1875   HRH Prince Leopold (afterwards Duke of Albany KG)

4 Nov 1875   Sir George Biddell Airy KCB, DCL, LL.D, FRS, etc., Astronomer Royal

9 Mar 1876   Rt. Hon. Sir Alexander James Edmund Cockburn GCB, Lord Chief Justice of England

25 July 1876   His Excellency Sir Salar Jung GCSI, Prime Minister of the Nizam of Hyderabad

15 June 1877   General Ulysses Grant, late President of the USA
[voted the honorary freedom on 31 May 1877, and attended Guildhall on 15 June 1877, but as an alien he could not take the oath of allegiance to the British crown, and thus he was technically not admitted to the city freedom]

3 Aug 1878   Rt. Hon. Benjamin Disraeli, Earl of Beaconsfield, Prime Minister of England

     Most Hon. Robert Arthur Talbot Gascoyne Cecil, Marquis of Salisbury KG, HM Secretary of State for Foreign Affairs

6 June 1879   Sir Rowland Hill KCB, etc.

6 Oct 1880   Sir Henry Bessemer FRS, MICE

14 Feb 1881   Major-General Sir Frederick Sleigh Roberts GCB, VC

13 Oct 1881   Rt. Hon. William Ewart Gladstone MP, Prime Minister of England
[had been previously admitted by redemption through the Turners' Company on 17 March 1876]

11 Apr 1883	Admiral Sir Frederick Beauchamp Paget Seymour GCB (admitted as the Rt. Hon. Admiral Lord Alcester GCB)
20 June 1884	Rt. Hon. Anthony Ashley-Cooper, Earl of Shaftesbury KG, DCL
29 June 1885	HRH Prince Albert Victor of Wales KG
13 Jan 1887	Henry Morton Stanley [explorer: although in fact a British subject, he was generally regarded as being an American citizen and was therefore not called upon to make the declaration of a freeman]
18 Apr 1888	Rt. Hon. the Marquis of Hartington MP
29 May 1889	Most Hon. Frederick Temple, Marquis of Dufferin and Earl of Ava KP, GCB, GCSI, GCMG
1 June 1889	HRH Prince George of Wales KG
6 May 1891	William Lidderdale, Governor of the Bank of England
26 Sep 1893	Sir John Gilbert RA
4 June 1894	George Williams [philanthropist, awarded the honorary city freedom for his work for the young men of the city and for the YMCA, in its 50th anniversary year]
11 July 1895	Rt. Hon. Arthur Wellesley Peel MP, Speaker of the House of Commons (admitted as the Rt. Hon. Viscount Peel)
4 Nov 1898	Major-General Sir Herbert Kitchener KCB, KCMG (admitted as the Rt Hon. Horatio Herbert, Lord Kitchener of Khartoum and Aspall KCB, KCMG, RE)
20 July 1899	John Henniker Heaton MP
11 July 1901	Colonel Sir James Willcocks KCMG, DSO
23 July 1901	Rt. Hon. Lord Milner (admitted as the Rt. Hon. Alfred, Baron Milner GCB, GCMG)
20 July 1904	His Excellency the Rt. Hon. Lord Curzon of Kedleston GMSI, GMIE, Viceroy of India
10 Oct 1905	Rt. Hon. William Court Gully, Viscount Selby, Speaker of the House of Commons
26 Oct 1905	Rev. William Booth
16 Apr 1907	Rt. Hon. Sir Wilfrid Laurier PC, GCMG, Prime Minister of Canada
	Hon. Alfred Deakin, Prime Minister of Australia
	Hon. Sir Joseph Ward KCMG, Prime Minister of New Zealand
	Hon. Dr. Leander Starr Jameson CB, Prime Minister of Cape Colony

Hon. Frederick Robert Moor, Prime Minister of Natal

General the Hon. Louis Botha, Prime Minister of the Transvaal

1 May 1907   Rt. Hon. Sir Robert Bond PC, KCMG, Prime Minister of Newfoundland

28 June 1907   Rt. Hon. Lord Lister OM, MD, FRS, DCL

28 Oct 1907   Rt. Hon. Evelyn Baring, Earl of Cromer GCB, OM, GCMG, KCSI, CIE, LL.D

Miss Florence Nightingale OM
[voted the honorary city freedom on 13 Feb 1908, but she was too ill to attend, therefore a copy of the resolution was presented to Mr LH Shore Nightingale on 16 March 1908]

31 May 1910   The Hon. Theodore Roosevelt, ex-President of the USA
[voted the honorary freedom on 3 March 1910, and attended Guildhall on 31 May 1910, but as an alien he could not take the oath of allegiance to the British crown, and thus he was technically not admitted to the city freedom]

23 Feb 1911   Rt. Hon. Sir Gilbert Kynynmond, Earl of Minto KG, PC, GCSI, GCMG, GCIE, Viceroy of India

23 Jan 1912   Rt. Hon. Albert Henry George Grey, the Earl Grey GCB, GCMG, GCVO, Governor-General of Canada

29 July 1915   Rt. Hon. Sir Robert Laird Borden PC, GCMG, KC, DCL, LL.D, Prime Minister of Canada

18 April 1916   Rt. Hon. William Morris Hughes KC, Prime Minister of Australia

6 Nov 1916   Rt. Hon. William Ferguson Massey , Prime Minister of New Zealand

27 April 1917   Rt. Hon. David Lloyd George MP , Prime Minister

1 May 1917   Colonel His Highness Maharajah Sir Ganga Singh Bahadur of Bikaner GCSI, GCIE etc.

Lieutenant-General the Rt. Hon. Jan Christian Smuts KC

Rt. Hon. Sir Edward Patrick Morris KCMG, KC, Prime Minister of Newfoundland

Sir James Scorgie Meston KCSI , Lieutenant Governor of the United Provinces of Agra and Oudh

Sir Satyendra Prasanna Sinha, member designate of the Executive Council of Bengal

29 May 1919   HRH Edward Albert Christian George Andrew Patrick David, The Prince of Wales KG, GMMG, GMBE, MC (afterwards King Edward VIII)

12 June 1919   Admiral of the Fleet Sir David Beatty GCB, OM, GCVO, DSO

Field Marshal Sir Douglas Haig KT, GCB, OM, GCVO, KCIE

18 July 1919 General John Joseph Pershing GCB, Commander in Chief, American Expeditionary Forces
[voted the honorary freedom on 3 July 1919, and attended Guildhall on 18 July 1919, but as an alien he could not take the oath of allegiance to the British crown, and thus he was technically not admitted to the city freedom]

30 July 1919 Marshal Ferdinand Foch OM, Commander in Chief, Allied Forces
[voted the honorary freedom on 3 July 1919, and attended Guildhall on 30 July 1919, but as an alien he could not take the oath of allegiance to the British crown, and thus he was technically not admitted to the city freedom]

7 Oct 1919 General Sir Edmund Henry Hynman Allenby GCB, GCMG (admitted as Field Marshal the Rt. Hon. Viscount Allenby)

24 Oct 1919 General Armando Diaz, Commander in Chief, Italian Forces
[voted the honorary freedom on 11 September 1919, and attended Guildhall on 24 October 1919, but as an alien he could not take the oath of allegiance to the British crown, and thus he was technically not admitted to the city freedom]

28 Oct 1919 HRH Prince Albert Frederick Arthur George KG, Duke of York (afterwards King George VI)

17 May 1920 Admiral of the Fleet the Rt. Hon. John Rushworth Jellicoe, Viscount Jellicoe GCB, OM, GCVO

Field Marshal the Rt. Hon. John Denton Pinkstone French, Viscount French of Ypres PC, KP, GCB, OM, GCVO, KCMG

31 May 1921 HRH Prince Henry William Frederick Albert KG , Duke of Gloucester

15 July 1921 Rt. Hon. Arthur Meighen KC, Prime Minister of Canada

27 July 1921 His Highness Maharaja Dhiraj Mirza Maharao Shri Khengarji Savai Bahadur, Maharao of Kutch GCSI, GCIE

Hon. Valangimon Sankaranarayana Srinivasa Sastri

12 Oct 1923 Rt. Hon. Stanley Baldwin MP, Prime Minister
[had been previously admitted to the city freedom by redemption through the Goldsmiths' Company on 28 June 1904]

Rt. Hon. William Lyon Mackenzie King CMG, LL.D, Prime Minister of Canada

Rt. Hon. Stanley Melbourne Bruce MC, Prime Minister of Australia

14 Feb 1924 Rt. Hon. James William Lowther, Viscount Ullswater GCB, Speaker of the House of Commons

23 May 1924 HRH Prince George Edward Alexander Edmund KG, Duke of Kent

13 May 1925	Rt. Hon. Herbert Henry Asquith, Earl of Oxford and Asquith
25 Mar 1926	Rt. Hon. Sir Austen Chamberlain KG, MP, Secretary of State for Foreign Affairs
8 June 1926	Most Hon. Rufus Daniel, Marquis of Reading GCB, GCSI, GCIE, GCVO, Viceroy of India
19 Nov 1926	Rt. Hon. Joseph Gordon Coates MC, Prime Minister of New Zealand
	General the Hon. James Barry Munnik Hertzog, Prime Minister of South Africa
19 Nov 1926	Hon. Walter Stanley Monroe, Prime Minister of Newfoundland
22 Oct 1928	Most Rev. and Rt. Hon. Randall Thomas Davidson GCVO, DD, DCL, LL.D, Lord Archbishop of Canterbury
18 Oct 1929	Lieutenant-General the Rt. Hon. Lord Baden-Powell GCMG, GCVO, KCB, LL.D, FRGS
19 Dec 1929	Rt. Hon. James Ramsay MacDonald MP, Prime Minister
	Rt. Hon. Philip Snowden MP, Chancellor of the Exchequer
4 Nov 1930	Rt. Hon. Richard Bedford Bennett KC, LL.D, MP, Prime Minister of Canada
	Rt. Hon. James Henry Scullin MP, Prime Minister of Australia
	Rt. Hon. George William Forbes MP, Prime Minister of New Zealand
23 July 1935	Colonel and Alderman the Rt. Hon. Viscount Wakefield CBE [had been previously admitted to the city freedom by redemption through the Haberdashers' Company on 12 February 1904]
14 June 1937	Rt. Hon. Joseph Aloysius Lyons CH, Prime Minister of Australia
14 June 1937	Rt. Hon. Michael Joseph Savage, Prime Minister of New Zealand
27 Oct 1937	Alderman Sir George Wyatt Truscott [had been previously admitted to the city freedom by patrimony through the Stationers' Company on 5 November 1878]
19 Dec 1940	Rt. Hon. Neville Chamberlain MP [voted the honorary Freedom on 6 October 1938, but died before he could be admitted: resolution presented to his widow]
30 June 1943	Rt. Hon. Winston Spencer Churchill CH, MP, Prime Minister
10 May 1944	Rt. Hon. John Curtin, Prime Minister of Australia
	Rt. Hon. Peter Fraser, Prime Minister of New Zealand
12 June 1945	General of the Army Dwight David Eisenhower GCB, Supreme Commander, Allied Expeditionary Force

[voted the honorary freedom on 24 May 1945, and attended Guildhall on 12 June 1945, but as an alien he could not take the oath of allegiance to the British crown, and thus he was technically not admitted to the city freedom]

19 Mar 1946   Field Marshal the Rt. Hon. Viscount Alexander of Tunis GCB, GCMG, CSI, DSO, MC, ADC

28 May 1946   Marshal of the Royal Air Force the Rt. Hon. Lord Tedder GCB

12 June 1946   Admiral of the Fleet the Rt. Hon. Viscount Cunningham of Hyndhope KT, GCB, DSO

Field Marshal the Rt. Hon. Viscount Alanbrooke GCB, DSO

Marshal of the Royal Air Force the Rt. Hon. Viscount Portal of Hungerford GCB, OM, DSO, MC

10 July 1946   Admiral Lord Louis Mountbatten GCVO, KCB, DSO

18 July 1946   Field Marshal the Rt. Hon. Viscount Montgomery of Alamein GCB, DSO

11 June 1947   HRH Princess Elizabeth Alexandra Mary [afterwards Queen Elizabeth II]

8 June 1948   HRH Prince Philip, Duke of Edinburgh KG

4 June 1952   Rt. Hon. Robert Gordon Menzies CH, QC, Prime Minister of Australia

28 Oct 1953   HM Queen Elizabeth the Queen Mother

20 Nov 1953   Rt. Hon. Clement Richard Attlee OM, CH, MP

7 Feb 1955   Rt. Hon. Louis Stephen St Laurent QC, Prime Minister of Canada

3 July 1956   Jawaharlal Nehru, Prime Mininster of India
[not called upon to make the declaration of a freeman]

Rt. Hon. Sidney George Holland, Prime Minister of New Zealand

15 Dec 1961   Rt. Hon. Harold Macmillan MP, Prime Minister

25 Feb 1963   Rt. Hon. John Diefenbaker QC, Prime Minister of Canada

21 June 1966   HRH Princess Margaret, Countess of Snowden CI, GCVO

27 Nov 1967   Rt. Hon. Lester Bowles Pearson OBE, Prime Minister of Canada

18 June 1968   Rt. Hon. Yang Teramat Mulia Tunku Abdul Rahman Putra Al-Haj KOM, CH, Prime Minister of Malaysia

17 Jan 1969   Rt. Hon. Keith Jacks Holyoake CH, Prime Minister of New Zealand

2 Mar 1971   HRH Prince Charles, Prince of Wales KG

13 Mar 1975   Rt. Hon. Pierre Elliott Trudeau, Prime Minister of Canada

12 Dec 1975   Rt. Hon. Harold Wilson OBE, MP, Prime Minister

27 Feb 1976   HRH Princess Anne Elizabeth Alice Louise, Mrs Mark Phillips GCVO

15 July 1982   Lee Kuan Yew GCMG, CH, Prime Minister of Singapore

22 July 1987   HRH Diana Frances, Princess of Wales

26 May 1989   Rt. Hon. Margaret Thatcher FRS, MP, Prime Minister

10 July 1996   Nelson Mandela, President of South Africa
[not called upon to make the declaration of a freeman]

18 Feb 1998   Helmut Kohl, Federal Chancellor of Germany
[not called upon to make the declaration of a freeman]

APPENDIX 5
BOYD'S INHABITANTS OF LONDON

One way in which many people first discover that their ancestors were freemen of the city of London or of one of its livery companies is through Boyd's Inhabitants of London (238 volumes) held at the SoG, together with its index (27 volumes). Guildhall Library also has a microfilm copy of the index only. It is often found cited in older reference works under its former name of Boyd's *Citizens of London,* a name no longer used, as the *Inhabitants of London* is much more wide-ranging in its contents than just freemen (implied by the word 'citizens') of London.

The *Inhabitants of London* was begun in 1935 by Percival Boyd, who intended to draw together on 'unit sheets' details of family groups from all kinds of different records. Information on the sheets was to include dates of birth and/or baptism, marriage, death and/or burial, plus residence, names of parents, marriage partners, children and their marriage partners, and livery company. The proposed country-wide scheme was a failure, but the scheme was a success for the London area, for which Boyd produced in his own lifetime some 59,389 family group sheets, containing information gleaned from an immense number of sources, both printed and manuscript. The *Inhabitants of London* is fullest for the 16th and 17th centuries, although contains entries from the 15th to the 19th centuries. Boyd presented his work to the SoG in 1939, although he retained it for his own use, happily making searches for enquirers, during his lifetime. The *Inhabitants of London* complements and often overlaps with Boyd's *Marriage index* and *Index of London burials,* which are also held at the SoG. For further details about Boyd's *Inhabitants of London,* see John Beach Whitmore 'London citizens' in *Genealogists' Magazine* Vol. 9 (March 1944) p. 385 and Anthony J Camp 'Boyd's London burials and citizens of London' in *Family Tree* Vol. 1, No. 6 (Sep/Oct 1985).

The indexes include name, dates of marriage and death and the family sheet number. The family sheets can be extremely informative, as shown in the example in plate X. The reference in plate X to a 'Com Serj Index' is one which occurs fairly frequently throughout the sheets and refers to the indexes to the common serjeants' books in CLRO. The common serjeant presided over the court of orphans, which administered the personal estate of deceased freemen and produced inventories of their personal property (not land, or real property: see chapter 2 under 'rights and privileges' for details). When Boyd was working, the only finding aids which

Name _James Clutterbuck_ of _____

Father _Richard Clutterbuck 610_ of _S Peter West cheap 13978_

Mother _Anne Brand_ of _S Martin le Grand_

daughter of _John Brand_ and _____

Born _1607_ at _____

Married _1657 June 20_ at _Saffron Walden Essex + 9? Chesterford_

Wife _Margaret Reynolds_ of _Helions Bumsted Essex_

Born _____ at _____ Died _____ at _____

daughter of _James Reynolds_ and _____

Educated _____

Profession etc. _citizen + draper free 1631 Jan 11 by John Clutterbuck_
warden 1664 surety for J.C. apt Anne Huxley £200
Com Serj Index II 202 + widow Margaret orphans Anne Dorothy

Died _1672 Dec 24_ Buried at _S Vedast_

Will _admon P C C 1672 Jan 10 to widow Margaret_

Children

Anne   1658 _marr 1677 Anthony Crackrode   54610_

Dorothy _marr 1680 James Duncan   18191_

Plate X: Typical Family Sheet, of James Clutterbuck (1607-72, married 1657) from Boyd's Inhabitants of London [SoG reference: Boyd's Inhabitants of London: sheet 18197]

enabled researchers to find orphans' inventories in CLRO were the indexes to the common serjeants' books, but these have now been amended to allow quicker access to the actual inventories without having to look at the common serjeants' books first. In the case of James Clutterbuck in plate X, Boyd has clearly seen the index to common serjeants' book 2, folio 302v ('Com Serj Index II 302b') at CLRO, which does indeed name 'James Cloterbuck', his widow Margaret and his two underage daughters Anne and Dorothy. In this case, however, it appears that Boyd did not look at common serjeant's book 2, folio 302v itself, which also gives an address for James Clutterbuck ('Broad Streete, in Adam Court'). Clutterbuck's orphans' inventory at CLRO [orphans' inventory 825] contains a full inventory of his household goods, room by room, and debts owed and owing at the time of his death.

Another reference which turns up repeatedly in Boyd's *Inhabitants of London* is to 'LB', which stands for the letter books, also held by CLRO (see chapter 1 for details). The letter books 1275-1498 have been edited by RR Sharpe and published by the Corporation of London in 11 volumes (see appendix 1 for details).

APPENDIX 6
USEFUL ADDRESSES

British Library Newspaper Library
Colindale Avenue
London NW9 5HE

Chamberlain's Court
PO Box 270
Guildhall
London EC2P 2EJ

Corporation of London Records Office (CLRO)
PO Box 270
Guildhall
London EC2P 2EJ

Guildhall Library [including Bookshop and Printed Books and Manuscripts Sections]
Aldermanbury
London EC2P 2EJ

Public Record Office (PRO)
Ruskin Avenue
Kew
Richmond
Surrey KT9 4DU

Society of Genealogists
14 Charterhouse Buildings
Goswell Road
London EC1M 7BA

NOTES AND REFERENCES

1 Framework Knitters' Company register of freedom admissions 1713-1724, Guildhall Library Manuscripts Section reference: MS 3445/1, p.141.

2 Report of the general purposes (common council) committee to the court of common council, presented 30 June 1801, CLRO reference: printed report B/30D.

3 City freedom admission papers of Germaine Lavie, free of the city in January 1749/50, CLRO reference: CF 1/738. The author is indebted to Peter Clark for bringing this example, and the proof of age, to her attention.

4 Petition of John Hunter to the court of aldermen 7 February 1694/5, CLRO references: Rep 99 (1), p.348 and Misc MSS 18.35.

5 City freedom admission papers of Frances Ludlow, free of the city in April 1804, CLRO reference: CF1/1283/60-61.

6 Sharpe, RR, ed. *Calendar of letter book D (1309-13 14)* (London, 1902) p.vii.

7 Order of the court of common council 20 February 5 Hen. VI [1427], CLRO reference: journal 2, f. 90r.

8 Order of the court of common council 26 October 16 Eliz.I [1574], CLRO reference: journal 20, part 1, f 176v *et seq*.

9 Proceedings of the court of common council 2 September 29 Hen. VIII [1537], CLRO reference: journal 14, f. 41r.

10 Proceedings of the court of common council 1 August 1609, CLRO reference: journal 27, f.385v.

11 Proceedings of the court of common council 29 January 1746/7, and 15 December 1747, CLRO references: journal 59, ff.62v-64r, 105v-107r.

12 Petition of John Benjamin Tolkien to the court of common council on 22 April 1813, CLRO references: common council minutes 1813, p.32; journal 87, pp.502-503 and city freedom admission papers for April 1813, CLRO reference: CF1/1383.

13 Petitions of Peter Augustus Stocqueler, Lewis de Beaune and William George

Rolfes to the court of common council on 11 May and 17 June 1813, CLRO references: common council minutes 1813, pp.38, 45; journal 88, ff.43 r-v, 44 r-v, 74v-75r.

14 Order of the court of common council 18 May 1916, CLRO reference: common council minutes 1916, p.140.

15 Order of the court of common council 8 February 1917, common council minutes 1917, p.42.

16 Order of the court of common council 30 April 1953 (on the recommendation of the committee of the whole court of common council), CLRO references: common council minutes 1953, p.145 and printed report C/71.

17 Proceedings of the court of aldermen 7 and 14 September 1731 CLRO references: repertory 135, pp.451, 475 and city freedom admission papers of John Satia, free of the city September1731, CLRO reference: CF 1/520.

18 Case for opinion relating to the admission of Quakers to the freedom of the city of London, 1713, CLRO reference: Cases relating to the city of London (1 volume, (250A)), case 42, ff.31v-34r.

19 Papers relating to the case of Richard Pierce, city's tenant collector of the package and scavage dues, about 1684-1726, CLRO reference. Misc MSS 42.2.

20 Proceedings of the court of common council 3 February and 2 March 1737/8, CLRO references: journal 58, ff.70v, 73v.

21 Act of common council 10 December 1830, CLRO references: [common council minutes 1830, pp.170-171] and court of aldermen papers, 22 Feb 1831.

22 City freedom book entry for the city freedom admission of Joseph Lewis, free of the city 1 February 1831, CLRO reference: CF2/23.

23 Act of parliament for regulating elections in the city of London, 1849 (12 & 13 Vict, cap.94, para. 10), CLRO reference: PD 2.7.

24 CLRO reference: GLMS 512.

25 British Library reference: Egerton MS 2408.

26 City freedom admission papers relating to the recording of the change of name of Thomas Piggott, *alias* Benson in August 1719, CLRO reference: CF1/380/75-76. There are also references to this case being considered by the

court of aldermen in repertory 123, pp.200 (10 Feb 1718/9) and 462 (30 June 1719).

27 Order of the court of common council 20 December 1899, CLRO reference: common council minutes 1899, p.448.

28 CLRO reference: CIV/1/1 0.

29 Order of the court of common council 19 September 1918, CLRO reference: common council minutes 1918, p.210.

30 Proceedings of the court of common council 25 March and 21 October 1920, CLRO references: common council minutes 1920, pp.129, 378.

31 Proceedings of the court of common council 10 December 1920, CLRO reference: common council minutes 1920, p.449

32 Proceedings of the court of common council 21 April 1921, CLRO references: common council minutes 1921, p.134 and printed report C/18W.

33 CLRO reference: printed report C/18W.

34 Order of the court of common council 3 June 1920, CLRO reference: common council minutes 1920, p.190.

35 Proceedings of the court of common council 26 October 1920, CLRO references: common council minutes 1920, pp.381, 403 and general purposes (common council) committee minutes, volume 69, pp.8-9, 19.

36 Proceedings of the court of common council 20 May 1915, CLRO reference: common council minutes 1915, p.142.

37 Order of the court of common council 12 July 1945, CLRO reference: common council minutes 1945, p.132.

38 City freedom admission papers of John Adams, free of the city December 1690, CLRO reference: ELJL/41/1.

39 City freedom admission papers of Richard Fauston, free of the city March 1821, CLRO reference: CF1/1470/13(a).

40 City freedom admission papers of Edward Fisher, free of the city October 1764, CLRO reference: CF1/912/125.

41 Entries relating to Edward Fisher in Guildhall Library Manuscripts Section

microfilm of Bridewell and Bethlem court of governors' minute book 1762-1781, pp.97, 128, 140, 183.

42 Alfred James Copeland *Bridewell Royal Hospital past and present* (London 1888) p.101.

43 Letter drafted on the back of the city freedom admission paper of John Townsend, free of the city June 1691, CLRO reference: ELJL/47/98 (dorse).

44 Turnover memorandum, part of city freedom admission papers of Henry Bateman, free of the city January 1824, CLRO reference: CF1/1501/2c.

45 Turnover memorandum, part of the city freedom admission papers of Joseph Lamb, free of the city October 1767, CLRO reference: CF1/948.

46 Apprenticeship indenture, part of the city freedom admission papers of Joseph Lamb, free of the city October 1767, CLRO reference: CF 1/948.

47 City freedom admission papers of George Thomas, free of the city November 1764, CLRO reference: CF1/913/7.

48 Richard Younge's *The heart's index* exists in many editions. Editions of 1659, 1664, 1665 and 1667 are listed as entries Y157-Y160 in Donald Wing's *Short-title catalogue of books published in England ... [and elsewhere] 1641-1700,* Vol. 3 (New York, 1988). Editions of 1711, 1739 and 1776 are held by Guildhall Library.

49 Re-used printed page, forming the back of the city freedom admission paper of John Chapman, free of the city August 1697, CLRO reference: ELJL/120/91 (dorse). The author is indebted to Ivy Sharp for bringing this item to her attention.

50 City freedom admission paper of Joseph Webb, free of the city June 1691, CLRO reference: ELJL/47/99.

51 City freedom admission papers of John Lowder, free of the city November 1764, CLRO reference: CF1/913/3.

52 City freedom admission papers of Robert Winder, free of the city April 1731, CLRO reference: CF1/51 5/143 (a-c).

53 City freedom admission papers of George Shaw, free of the city September 1884 and Henry Ailwyn Shaw, free of the city October 1884, CLRO references:

CF1/2235 and CF1/2236 respectively. The author would like to thank Mr J Carnaby, Citizen and Plumber of London, for bringing this example to her notice.

[54] City freedom admission papers of Charles George Nottage, free of the city 8 January 1885, CLRO reference: CF 1/2239.

[55] City freedom admission papers of Harry Higgs, free of the city 4 May 1909, CLRO reference: CF1/253 0.

[56] City freedom admission papers of George Steaney, free of the city April 1730, CLRO reference: CF1/503 (old no. 27).

[57] City freedom admission papers of John Whitfield, free of the city April 1804, CLRO reference: CF1/1283/56.

INDEX